Building an Aviary

By

Robert G. Black

Avian Publications
6380 Monroe St NE
Minneapolis MN 55432

Bruce Burchett, Publisher
www.avianpublications.com
bruce@avianpublications.com
Phone & fax 763-571-8902

ISBN 0-910335-03-6

Printed in the USA

Dedication

This book is dedicated to the memory of

George A. Johnson
January 1, 1930 - April 5, 1995

He personified the positive traits of patience and
perseverance outlined in these pages. His careful planning,
meticulous execution, and successful projects, including an aviary,
over the years impressed this author as notable examples of human
thought, ingenuity and creativity.

Acknowledgements

The author owes an untold number of writers, aviculturists, fanciers, breeders and retailers for the knowledge and experience that has resulted in the publication of this book. However, a number of recent comments and also direct contributions of material and information have been instrumental in solidifying the idea for this book, and enabling the author to bring together the information in its present form.

First, my thanks to Crawford & Company for the employment that kept body and soul together when writing and aviculture alone could not. Though surely there are those individuals who breed and sell birds in sufficient quantities that no outside employment is necessary, it is rare indeed to actually find one! Most of us must work at some occupation far removed from the maintenance and breeding of cage birds.

Steve and Tami Payne of Livermore, California, were also very helpful in supplying information and the benefit of their years of breeding experience with a number of different avian families.

John Wilson of San Francisco, California, has the distinction of being the driving force (more correctly, the gentle, badgering force) that returned my activities and writing to the mainstream of aviculture.

Roy Beckham of San Jose, California, has shown how very much can be accomplished with the judicious use of patience and perseverance, those two primary requirements if you expect any success at all in the pursuit of aviculture.

CONTENTS

JAVA SPARROW
(*Munia oryzivora*)
wild form ♂ white var. ♀

An illustration from A. G. Butler's 1899 classic
Foreign Finches in Captivity, Second Edition

Introduction

Background and Basics

Aviaries have been a part of the human experience for thousands of years. The love of birds and the desire to keep them in good health and to raise them successfully is as old as civilization. Yet aviaries have never been a necessity for human life, other than the obvious need for keeping domesticated fowl as a food source. Considerable wealth was necessary for much of human history for anyone to be able to establish an aviary of exotic species just for the pleasure and the knowledge that would result. However, by the twentieth century anyone in the middle class of economic success could afford to have an aviary. Following the discovery of many new species and the classification of birds that continued from the eighteenth century until the present day, interest in the maintenance and breeding of exotic species increased dramatically.

However, with the occupational specialization that is so characteristic of the twentieth century, many people who wanted to establish an aviary and keep exotic birds had no idea how to go about this. The basic requirement for some kind of wire mesh over a framework that anyone understands, when actually put into practice can result in anything from an eye-catching masterpiece to a total failure. All of us are not carpenters, nor metalworkers, nor architects, and anyone born and raised in a city apartment building cannot begin to understand the requirements that must be met for the establishment of an aviary in the open countryside. As the author's experience ranges everywhere from apartment living in downtown Washington, D. C., to carving a homestead out of the vastness of interior Alaska, and every climate area from the Florida Keys to the Alaskan tundra, the benefit of that experience was vital to the creation of this booklet. By understanding and following the simple outlines included in this booklet, you will be able to plan and to build a safe and effective aviary for your birds no matter where you live.

Building an aviary requires knowledge in a variety of fields, and experience in even more fields to keep it operating and successful through all weather conditions and all of the living and intrinsic factors that are constantly working to destroy the birds and the aviary in which you keep them. That the experience is available for you here in this volume is a result of many past failures, more than an average number of minor disasters, and the author's monumental stubbornness and inability to accept anything as either 'natural' or as 'the only sensible way to do it'. This is a world of cause and effect that we live in, and every effect has a cause, and every action an effect. If the birds are not doing well in the aviary or not breeding as expected, there has to be a reason for that failure. Failure doesn't 'just happen' – failure is caused.

Most inexperienced breeders assume that an aviary is for keeping the birds from escaping. Though this is true, it is only part of its function. Equally as important for the health and safety of the birds is the need for shelter during inclement weather conditions. Even more important, an aviary serves to keep the natural predators and domesticated pets out of the aviary. Any aviary you build that does not fulfill all of these purposes will certainly not be a successful aviary. Murphy's Law will ensure that anything that can possibly go wrong in the aviary will go wrong, sooner or later. My own successes and also the unfortunate experiences and utter failures in my own aviaries are the basis for the information in this booklet that will show you how to build a safe and useful aviary most effectively for your own birds.

Aviaries can be located either indoors or outdoors. Construction of an aviary indoors usually requires that the size of the aviary be smaller, simply because of the lack of available space for a large aviary indoors. Nevertheless, a small aviary can be placed in an unused corner quite successfully. Also, if your home is large enough to have an enclosed atrium or greenhouse, these locations are excellent for a small aviary of exotic birds. Since indoor aviaries can be the source of a huge amount of dust, seed husks, odors and feathers, indoor aviary construction will require some forethought and planning. There are a variety of ways to reduce the spread of these aviary by-products, and these are covered in detail in Chapter 13.

Since most aviaries will be out of doors, most of the chapters in this booklet will stress the methods of outdoor construction. In any type of aviary construction, there is no substitute for a plan. You need first to plan the location of the aviary, then the size of the aviary, and last, the shape desired and the construction materials that you will need for the aviary. If you have a set budget for this construction, you will need to learn the prices for each item required for the construction of the aviary in order to be able to estimate the ultimate cost of the construction accurately. If the cost for the size you want exceeds your budget, you have two choices; either wait until you do have enough funds to cover the cost of the aviary construction, or reduce the size and complexity of the aviary so that the construction will fit within your budget.

This booklet will show you how to do this and will cover the items that are needed for a successful aviary in detail. There are always a variety of alternatives to any of the details of aviary construction, and nothing can be more frustrating than discovering that something important has been completely left out only after the aviary construction is finished. If something does not seem to be working out as you expected, look for an alternative way of doing the same thing that will work under your conditions. In constructing your aviary, you will find that flexibility is a key to your success. Though this includes your physical flexibility, it is far more important to be mentally flexible. Being able to change your way of thinking and to alter your plans in mid-stream is not just important for building an aviary, it is vital for your physical and economic survival.

We learn very little from an easy life in which everything goes perfectly. The greatest lessons are learned when we make a monumental blunder and have to suffer the consequences for it. Though this is certainly no fun, we all learn very valuable lessons from our worst mistakes. You learn very little when everything goes perfectly. True learning comes from the problems we encounter, the challenges we face, and the blunders and mistakes we make as we go through life. When we turn our efforts to the care and breeding of avian species, the possibilities for problems and mistakes multiply geometrically. Murphy's Law kicks in with full force, and everything that can possibly go wrong sooner or later will go wrong. The most important thing to remember is that mistakes are a part of life, they are human, and they are absolutely normal. Yet, without these constant problems and challenges, life would be very dull indeed. What will distinguish the successful person from the crowd is the assiduous cultivation and use of patience and perseverance to overcome any of the mistakes or obstacles that knock us flat.

A perfect example of the need for this patience and perseverance is the *Dictionary of the Finches and Seed-eating Birds* that the author is working on concurrently with this book that you are reading. Though there are only some 700 birds that are seed-eating birds with fairly stout beaks for the shelling of seeds, the number of names that have been used for these birds over the years since their discovery is nearly mind-boggling. The basic dictionary has smaller type than you are now reading, with minimal margins on each 8½ by 11 inch page. The basic dictionary already numbers over 1800 pages, with another 200 pages of appendices. I have worked on compiling this dictionary for a number of years, and have at least several more years of this work to do before the result will be anything close to a stage of completion and accuracy that will enable a publisher to seriously consider it.

Anyone who has ever tackled a similar project knows full well how much patience and perseverance this project has required and will continue to require for the foreseeable future. Nevertheless, with one step at a time, one fact at a time, it is possible to create a thoroughly detailed and comprehensive study of any subject you choose. If you can only answer one question each day, it will be amazing to look back at the end of a year and see how much you have been able to accomplish.

This Earth School that we attend each day so diligently, primarily since we wake up each day with no choice in the matter, is certainly a good place to learn, but it is also a merciless teacher and very unforgiving of mistakes that we make with our birds. Each of us has created many obligations that we must fulfill each day in our families, jobs, hobbies, and even recreations. When we also tackle aviculture and the breeding of any non-native avian species in captivity, we multiply those obligations. While the true needs of the birds are relatively simple, providing those needs is not simple, and many breeders and fanciers even seem to choose to make bird keeping far more complicated and frustrating than it really needs to be.

While you read this book, be aware of all of the problems that have been encountered, defined and overcome successfully to enable the author to supply you with this information and the benefit of many years of aviary experience. If the information presented here can keep you from the heartache of breeding failures and dead birds with just one species in just one area, it has served its purpose well.

As a final introductory note, the scientific name of a bird is included in this book the first time a species is mentioned. After that, the scientific name is usually omitted, except possibly for a few unusual avian species with which most readers will not be familiar at all. Looking up a bird by its common name alone is often quite a lengthy chore. Most birds have more than one common name, and some have several common names that are in use in the English speaking countries. The scientific name consists of a generic name to place the bird in a group of similar birds, then a species name that will separate this bird from all other similar birds. The scientific species name, once the ornithologists have settled on it, usually remains stable. Though the generic name may change as new information comes to light, the genus name and classification does not normally change for most birds.

However, research in the new fields of knowledge developed in the late 20th century caused recent revisions in the status and the names for many of the birds of the world. Three men in the 1970's and 1980's studied avian specimens from an entirely new perspective: protein electrophoresis and DNA analysis. Charles G. Sibley and Jon E. Ahlquist in 1975 began making major revisions in the then existing taxonomic structure, which is the naming system for the birds, based on their techniques of DNA-DNA hybridization. In 1983, Burt L. Monroe, Jr., began the huge job of correlating and computerizing this information.

Sibley and Monroe in 1990 published a book based on this new knowledge titled *Distribution and Taxonomy of Birds of the World*. They followed this in 1993 with *A World Checklist of Birds*. Though the family Psittacidae (the parrots), as an example, survived with only minor generic changes, the families set up to classify the finches and the other seed-eating birds were completely transformed, expanded and reorganized into only two avian families: Passeridae and Fringillidae. As a result, the scientific names for many of the birds are still in turmoil, with some ornithologists still favoring the old traditional taxonomic system, some solidly supporting the new Sibley-Monroe system, and the rest of the ornithologists favoring parts of both. It will be many years before the scientific names of the birds are again as stable as they were before 1990.

Chapter 1

Outdoor Aviaries
Planning for Everything

Building an outdoor aviary requires a lot of forethought and planning for a variety of weather conditions, as well as planning and allowing for a variety of avian species. For example, there is a very large difference in the construction requirements of an aviary designed for cockatoos and macaws as opposed to an aviary for softbills, doves and finches. An aviary for ground dwelling birds will have to be designed somewhat differently from an aviary that is being designed for hummingbirds. Most of the aviculturists reading this volume will need an aviary that can be adapted to a variety of uses and to a variety of avian species.

There are both advantages and disadvantages to keeping your birds in outdoor aviaries. The results of my experience and experimentation, however, indicate that the advantages of an outdoor aviary far outweigh the disadvantages. All birds will be healthier and will breed better when they are maintained outdoors in the sunlight, wind and rain. These are their natural habitat, and there are no better cleaning agents and disinfectants than these natural and changing weather conditions. The care and maintenance time required are reduced dramatically, by 90% or more, when the birds can be kept in larger groups in large, outdoor flights, rather than in indoor, labor-intensive cages.

The location of the aviary will be the first major decision you will have to make before beginning the construction planning. Most aviculturists will have a very limited choice of locations, unless you happen to live on a large acreage farm or ranch with almost unlimited possibilities. The potential locations may be sunny or shady, sloping or flat, or sandy or rocky, and the aviary must fit into the available location without extensive landfill or other preparation.

The first and most basic recommendation is to place any outdoor aviary in an area in which it receives at least half a day of direct sunlight. An aviary placed in a completely shaded location remains too wet, dries out very slowly after a rain, and continually fosters the growth of many types of harmful fungi, bacteria, and other microorganisms. Remember that the spores for these dangerous fungi and other microorganisms float in the air constantly, and even air that seems clear to the eye will have, by actual count, from 40,000 to 60,000 living things floating in each cubic foot of that air. These myriad life forms are just waiting for the air to deposit them in a suitable location where they can begin to grow and reproduce. If your aviary remains constantly damp, that is a blanket invitation for fungi and microorganisms of all descriptions to land there and begin their life cycles.

The birds never look their healthiest in a totally shaded location, and those from dry climates will always suffer from the higher humidity and damp conditions that are endemic to heavily shaded areas. I learned this forcefully and unhappily again recently when trying to keep a pair of Desert Finches, *Rhodopechys obsoleta*, in a shady area. When unusual weather conditions presented us with an uninterrupted two-week period of rain and high humidity, both of the Desert Finches died. All of the other finches maintained in the same area and under the same conditions remained in perfect health. Desert Finches simply cannot tolerate long periods of rain and high humidity.

This does not mean that all of your birds should be exposed to the fullest range of adverse weather conditions at all times. They do need protected areas to seek shelter from both sunshine and rain when necessary. Covering one-third to one-half of the aviary to allow the birds to find protection from the sunshine, as well as from rain and cold temperatures, has proven over the years of my experimentation to be the best method in any mild climate zone. During any reasonable weather conditions, only the top of the aviary need be covered. This gives the birds, their food, and their nesting sites adequate protection, while still keeping the area open enough to dry out rapidly after a bad storm or an extended rainy period.

A fiberglass or plastic covering as a roof can be installed in a variety of colors and densities to let in or exclude as much light as you want. I usually prefer the opaque, white or light green fiberglass roofing. This comes in sheets as short as 8 feet and is easily attached with a special roofing nail that has a rubber ring around it to provide a water seal once the nail head compresses this seal against the fiberglass. Even on cloudy days, the area still stays quite light underneath this material, while on blistering hot days, the opaque fiberglass roofing allows the birds an escape from the sun that is equivalent to a light shade tree. The light green coloring of some of the fiberglass panels very closely simulates the lighting conditions that you can expect to find under a tree in an open area.

Metal roofing material is also available very inexpensively in sheets of 8 feet, 12 feet and even longer. This type of roofing totally blocks out the light, however, and for this reason, I do not recommend its use in aviaries. Nevertheless, these sheets of metal roofing material are without a doubt the cheapest method for roofing any shed or outbuilding that is currently available on the market.

There is another material that has more recently become available on the market, and it is also now available in the standard length roofing sheets. This is the clear, polycarbonate sheeting, and it is now becoming widely used as a material for the construction of greenhouses. As a covering for part of the aviary, it is also an ideal roofing material. This clear sheeting allows most of the wavelengths of natural sunlight to go through it, however, and this may not be ideal for an aviary in full sun in a hot climate that really needs some shading effect. Polycarbonate is available for other applications in all colors, however, and by the time you read this, you will be able to find sheets of this material that have been tinted to provide some shading effect. If you can only find the clear polycarbonate sheets, you can always use some type of nursery shade cloth or other material to provide some shade for the birds. In a pinch, you can just sprinkle pine needles over the clear polycarbonate sheeting to provide the shading effect temporarily.

Regardless of the material that you decide to use for the covered portion of the aviary, be sure to slope the roofing to ensure proper drainage when it rains. A flat roof is an invitation for water to puddle on the roofing and then to find a spot that is not well sealed to leak through. Invariably, such a leak will be right over your feeding station so that the food in the aviary is soaked through. Most birds will not touch food that is wet, unless that food is a simple soaked seed. Everything that you can do to prevent your birds' feed from becoming wet will be a good investment for the future. A simple one inch slope for each three feet of aviary roofing is sufficient to ensure adequate drainage, but one inch of slope for each foot will provide much better and faster drainage. A greater slope than one inch per foot for the roof will cause faster drainage, but it is not necessary for proper drainage in most areas of normal rainfall.

At this point, I would stress that the aviary wire or hardware cloth should be attached to the top of the aviary even where the aviary is to be covered with a roofing material. Such compounds as fiberglass become brittle with age, and a good, stiff wind can crack the fiberglass sheets and tear them off of the aviary. If there is no wire underneath this roofing material, you will lose all of your birds. The wire covering will not come loose or blow off, and an aviary that has lost its fiberglass roofing, leaving you with wet birds and soggy feeding stations, is far preferable to an aviary that has lost all of its birds in a wind storm.

Since the food containers must be kept dry at all times, a pole that is placed under the covering material with a tray of the food items fastened on top of the post offers the best way to protect the food supply from the weather and to supply the food items for any of the birds that are not exclusively ground-dwellers. You can still fasten perches and even nesting receptacles under this feeding area. The food that the birds scatter out on the ground will still be a considerable amount, and other birds will eat the food on the ground. This is particularly true when you keep Button Quail, *Coturnix chinensis*, Diamond Doves, *Geopelia cuneata*, and other similar ground-dwelling species in the aviary. The seed and soft food that falls to the ground and is not eaten will either sprout or decompose, as does any other food item that ends up on the ground uneaten. Of all the feeding methods I have tried, I have found this pole feeder to be by far the easiest to work with and the least wasteful of the food items that you are providing to your birds in the outdoor aviary.

An alternate method of feeding is to place the food items in ceramic dishes on the ground in the protected part of the aviary. Feeding on the ground is instinctive and natural for most seed-eating birds, as well as for many of the soft-billed birds, and unless a blowing rain fouls the dishes and spoils the food, there is very little waste in this method of feeding. Wind and rain often come together, however, and feeding dishes on the floor of the aviary, even a number of feet away from the open side of the aviary, are likely to get wet whenever a heavy rain hits the aviary.

As an additional bit of information from my experience, ceramic dishes are by far the easiest to clean of any of the types that are currently found on the market. Plastics and metals all require extensive scrubbing, and even with this scrubbing, they never seem to come completely clean. Both plastic and metal containers in a very short time will be permanently scratched or marred by the chemical action of the birds' droppings. The ceramic dishes, by contrast, clean easily and completely even when you use only your fingers in washing them. Though the ceramic dishes are usually more expensive than metal ones, and far more expensive than the plastic ones, they are well worth the initial added expense.

As water sources for the finches and other birds, you have several options. Placing containers on the ground is usually the cheapest and most effective means, as the birds expect to find water on the ground, and any splashing or spillage will seep into the ground immediately. A variety of effective water containers are manufactured especially for cage birds and aviaries. However, the waterers that are manufactured for backyard poultry and for farms are cheaper and much more solidly constructed. There are far more people who keep chickens and other farm poultry than there are aviculturists, and the far greater demand for these poultry items results in an economy of scale for all products of this type. This means that the water containers sold in such large quantities can be both cheaper and far more durably made.

You can also install a plastic water line into the aviary, or into an entire bank of aviaries with one outlet in each section. Many types of pipes and outlets are made that will work quite well, but a standard outdoor water faucet is probably the cheapest and best. When left at a steady drip into a shallow saucer, this standard faucet is as good as any other type available. This assures that the birds always have fresh water for both drinking and bathing, and you never have to do anything except throw any accumulated litter out of the shallow saucer each day. This is by far the easiest, cleanest, and safest method of watering the birds that I have yet been able to discover.

If your aviary is on even a slight slope, you can build a waterway that goes through the aviary, with a small pool and electrical recirculating pump at the end of the waterway. An underground pipe can carry the water back to the starting point of the waterway, so that the water continuously flows through the aviary in a manner that appears completely natural. This is especially attractive and effective if you can run the waterway through a bank of aviaries, with a pump at the end to return the water by an underground pipe to the first aviary in the line. If cleaning becomes necessary, the water can be drained out at the pump outlet, then the waterway refilled after the cleaning is completed.

In an outdoor aviary, the larger psittacines have powerful beaks that can bite through fine wire mesh, and with sufficient working and pressure, they can pull apart larger mesh wire. Fortunately, if adequate wood is available in the aviary, they will choose to shred the wood rather than the wire in most cases. These large birds need something to chew on and shred. That need to shred and chew is built into their nature, and every breeder of these large psittacines should be aware of that simple fact. I have heard one parrot breeder go so far as to say that this shredding of plant material is the main purpose of parrots in nature, as they return an incredible amount of plant material from the trees to the forest floor for recycling. The aviary you build for the large psittacine birds must also take that into consideration.

Most parrot breeders use the chain link fencing for their aviaries, since this serves the need for aviary wire for parrots admirably. This type of fencing is used everywhere, and again, the economies of scale cause this product to be produced in such huge quantities that the chain link fencing sells cheaply enough to be used for aviaries. The chain link fencing is strong enough that no psittacine beak can ever succeed in breaking it.

Outdoor aviaries may be concrete based, or they may have the local soil for their base. I have tried both methods, and have found that concrete as an aviary base is a useless waste of time and money. Concrete requires cleaning to look decent, and the birds' droppings will actually dissolve the concrete they touch and will leave a tiny depression on the concrete surface. When multiplied by dozens of droppings each day per bird over a period of weeks, months, and years, the concrete will become rough and unsightly and impossible to clean. In this condition, it becomes a breeding ground for dangerous microorganisms whose toxic by-products may be fatal to the birds in the aviary.

The concrete base of the aviary can be sealed and coated to prevent this from happening. If this is done, the concrete floor is much more easily cleaned and will last a lot longer. The surface friction is far less on sealed concrete, however, and when the concrete becomes wet or fouled with damp food or bird droppings, it can become exceedingly slippery and dangerous to anyone who is caring for the birds.

There is no better material than natural soil for the floor and base of an aviary. Though you must take a few minimal precautions to prevent wild and domesticated animals from digging into the aviary to harass and kill the birds. Refer to Chapter 5 for full coverage on the subject of varmint proofing for an aviary. The natural soil base effectively will recycle all bird droppings, seed hulls, eggs that are infertile or dead in the shell, and waste food products. Though the natural soil for the floor of the aviary may be a source of contamination with intestinal parasites, my own feeling is that this is so rare in good, fertile soil as to be negligible.

If you live in a desert area, this is the only place where you may have to add some moisture and to rake over the waste material to allow it to decompose naturally in the soil. Though the soil bacteria alone will do the job effectively, the most effective reclycler I have noted in the soil of an aviary is a good population of earthworms. In any area of regular rainfall, the earthworms that are found naturally in any moist soil will be the most effective recycling machine that you could possibly have. These earthworms will eat all of the waste organic matter on the floor of the aviary. Even a moist soil that is almost completely sand or gravel will still harbor a few earthworms. Those earthworms will be drawn to the organic waste material in any aviary, and they can eat and reprocess a huge amount of this material during the course of a 24-hour day.

Once you have a supply of earthworms in the soil, the earthworms will begin to breed and multiply rapidly. You will know that the earthworms are in your aviary in abundance when you see their perfectly round castings in any area that remains damp constantly. These are actually the egg casings, and each will hatch into one or more tiny earthworms that will continually replenish those that die or are eaten by the birds. It is well worthwhile to add earthworms to the soil in the bottom of your aviary if you don't have them already there naturally, and you can find small cartons of earthworms quite inexpensively and usually in several varieties at any location that sells fish bait.

In areas where the winter temperatures go far below freezing, you will need to take additional precautions to protect the birds and to ensure that they have adequate drinking water at all times. Snowfall must also be taken into consideration. Failing to adequately prepare for severe winter conditions will multiply your work in caring for the birds, even when they are hardy enough to take freezing temperatures without undue hardship or losses. Without proper care, even hardy birds are likely to succumb to the severe winter conditions that are all too likely in the more northern parts of our country and through most of Canada.

First, the slope of the roofing should be steep enough to allow snow to slide off when melting, or to allow you to push it off when low temperatures prevent the snow from melting. Snow is heavy, and an unexpected three or four foot snowfall will put enough weight on the covered portion of the aviary to break aviary supports and to pull the wire or hardware cloth loose from the framing. If you live in a high snowfall area, be sure to plan ahead for heavy snowfalls. The old tried and true method for avoiding the danger of snow weight and excess snow accumulation is a steep roof with a slope in excess of 45 degrees.

Besides the roofing problem, an outdoor aviary may need temporary covering on all sides to hold in and conserve the warmth of the aviary so that the temperature remains at least above freezing for your birds. A variety of clear and opaque materials are available for this purpose, and they have been used for both temporary and permanent siding on outdoor aviaries in northern climates for many years.

The first, and also the cheapest and easiest to install, is the standard clear polyethylene sheeting used for construction work. You can buy this at any building supply or home improvement center. This polyethylene sheeting can be fastened to the sides or the open top of an aviary rapidly and reasonably easily with short roofing nails or staples. Stapling with a hand or power stapler is the fastest method for installing and fastening down this polyethylene sheeting, and if the sheeting is folded over about a half an inch before stapling, the resulting covering of three layers of the polyethylene will be far more secure, especially under windy conditions. Where the sheet ends, a triple fold stapled every three or four inches will prevent the wind from tearing the polyethylene loose from the sides of the aviary. In order to prevent the wind from tearing this material loose, be sure to fasten all edges of the polyethylene sheeting with staples or short roofing nails.

The clear fiberglass or polycarbonate sheets are the next possibility for use as temporary winter siding for an outdoor aviary. These sheets are fairly inexpensive, and you can drill holes in them and fasten them down using bolts, nuts and washers so they are reusable for a number of years. The clear sheets will admit more light than the colored or opaque, white sheets, so they are the best type to use as a temporary winter covering on the sides of the aviary. Any large hardware or home improvement store carries the fiberglass sheets as a standard, stock item, though the polycarbonate sheets may be more difficult to find. In order to make your outdoor aviary warmer and to minimize cold air circulation and drafts, it is always a good idea to cover the portions of the aviary that are to receive the roofing sheets with a layer of the clear polyethylene plastic first. This will create a dead air space that will be of great importance in the heating of the aviary and the protection of the birds.

One note of warning if you are buying the wooden filler pieces for the ends of the sheets of fiberglass or polycarbonate. These products are fabricated by different manufacturers and at slightly different size specifications. *The wooden filler pieces for these sheets are not interchangeable.* Be sure to buy the wooden filler strips at the same place you buy the clear sheeting. Better yet, test one of the filler strips on one of the sheets to be sure they fit properly before you purchase them. Nothing is more exasperating than to be all ready to install the material and then find that the filler strips don't fit the sheeting you've installed.

Glass is an ideal temporary winter covering for the sides of a aviary, but it is considerably more expensive than the fiberglass or polycarbonate sheets. Since glass passes all except the ultraviolet wavelengths of light, the aviary will stay as bright during the winter as it is in the summer without the glass in place. You will need wooden edging or framing of some type to attach the glass to the side of the aviary, plus some form of insulation around the edges to prevent drafts of cold winter air. The main disadvantage to glass is the brittle quality of the material. Any sharp blow by a falling tree limb or a blowing metal trash can lid is likely to break it.

The thermal plastic sheets, usually referred to as Plexiglas®, also make a good winter covering for the sides of an aviary. Though sheets of this material are far more expensive than the previously discussed fiberglass and polycarbonate sheeting, they are also stiffer, more easily worked and drilled than glass, and they provide a more insulated winter covering for the sides of the aviary. Temporary wooden stays can be used to hold these sheets of thermal plastic in place, or you can drill holes in them and fasten them securely with bolts, nuts and washers. The primary disadvantages in using these thermal plastic sheets is in their high cost and in the fact that the material is not nearly so hard as glass, and it scratches very easily.

Keeping the water in liquid form in your aviaries during cold weather is also a vital necessity. Birds cannot get their needed water when the water containers are frozen solid. Worse, freezing water expands, and it will shatter glass water containers as it freezes. Freezing water will also crack plastic water containers, and it will break open galvanized containers at the seams, making them no longer usable. Removing the water each evening and replacing it in the morning can be effective if the daytime temperatures are going above freezing, but this is a great deal of unnecessary work, particularly when you may have dozens of outdoor aviaries in operation with a wide variety of birds in residence.

There are many different types of water heating elements on the market that are electrical and meant to be submerged in the drinking water to prevent it from freezing. These are very effective in large water containers used for livestock on a farm, but they are all too large and powerful for use in any small water container of the type that you will be using in an aviary. In a pinch, you could use one of these submersible heaters on a timer so that it was only on for ten minutes or so out of every hour. This would be sufficient to keep the water from freezing until you could get a better type of heater for use in your aviaries.

The electrical germination mats that are used in the nursery business are available in a variety of sizes, and you can place these under an avian water container to keep the temperature ten or more degrees above the outside temperature. Once the outside temperatures go to 10 degrees or so below freezing, however, these mats will not produce enough heat to keep the water from freezing. Also, they are made in sizes to fit the nursery flats that are so commonly seen in areas that sell bedding plants. None of the sizes manufactured are really small enough to place under a water container in an aviary, but they will serve the purpose until you can get something better to prevent your birds' water from freezing.

The best heating method I have found for a variety of water containers is a heater in the form of a round, electrically-wired metal base on which the water container sits. This electric heater base will keep the water from freezing even in temperatures in the 'teens on the Fahrenheit thermometer. Though several types are available, the best seems to be the metal base heater manufactured by Brower Equipment of Houghton, Iowa, U. S. A., and it uses only about 100 watts of power.

On areas of the aviary that are not covered with roofing material, remember that snow will still hold on the individual wires and will accumulate to the point where the weight is nearly as heavy as it is on the covered portions of the aviary. Alternate freezing and thawing will turn this snow into a heavy sheet of ice. Any roofing framing and wire that will not support the weight of this accumulated snow and ice will pull loose or break under the weight. This can easily result in a disaster that will cause you to lose all of the birds in the aviary.

Even if the wire and framing holds, when warmer temperatures come and the mass of accumulated snow and ice begins to thaw, dripping water everywhere in the aviary will turn the base of the aviary into a wet, soggy mess. Even in cold weather, a soggy, wet aviary is an invitation to spoiling and rot, and the proliferation of any variety of dangerous microorganisms.

Planning ahead for severe weather conditions will save you an inordinate amount of grief and extra work during the winter, when working, building and correcting mistakes can be the most uncomfortable for you, as well as for the birds. Chapter 8 covers the various methods you can use for heating the outdoor aviary if you live in an area of severe wintertime climates.

An aviary that is constructed on a flat location is usually the easiest to design and construct. You can make all of the corners square and then easily place the upright supports and roof supports at the correct distance to allow you to fasten the hardware cloth or poultry wire to these supports without extensive cutting and fitting. This type of aviary is the easiest and the fastest to construct, but it does end up with a boxy appearance. Having a bank of aviaries together sharing common sides except on the ends will make the appearance much more pleasing. Though this type of aviary is the easiest to build, it is also the least esthetically pleasing type of aviary.

On a fairly steep slope, you have two options. First, you can level the area for the aviary by terracing the slope. You will then, in effect, be building a square or box-type aviary on a flat surface, which is the least attractive type of aviary that you can build. Still, in order to eliminate this square appearance, you can merely make the part of the aviary on the upper hillside higher than the part of the aviary on the downhill side. By making the high side of the aviary 7½ feet tall and the low side 5½ feet tall, the aviary will still be basically the same size, but far more esthetically pleasing. Making the sides of the aviary different heights will give the appearance of an aviary that is built into the slope. This will also allow the aviary to blend with the slope in a more artistic and pleasing manner.

Alternately, you can design the aviary to fit into the slope of the hill, as discussed in more detail in Chapter 7 and illustrated on pages 62 and 63. This makes the aviary much more difficult and time consuming to construct, as many of the angles are not square, but are angles of thirty degrees or so to blend with the hillside slope. Cutting framing to this angle and then fastening it securely is a time-consuming job. Don't plan on building an aviary in this manner unless you are in no hurry whatsoever and can take your time to do the work carefully and to do it right.

Though this does make a very attractive aviary, more interior work is required to prevent the dirt of the hillside from slipping and sliding down to the low side of the aviary. Especially when you have quail, pheasants or other ground-dwelling birds in the aviary, their natural scratching for food constantly will cause dirt to be pushed to the bottom area of the aviary. Even finches will stir the soil enough to cause it to slide gradually to the low side of the aviary. Eventually, this soil will build up against the aviary wire, and it is not inconceivable that the birds could dig their way out of the aviary on the high side.

Terracing is one way to prevent the soil from being pushed to the low side of the sloping aviary. Terracing a slope takes quite a bit of time and effort, but the result will be well worth the effort. You will have a series of level surfaces held in place by the terracing material. If you live in an area where natural rocks are plentiful, you can use these to good advantage to create a series of terraces that appears perfectly natural within the aviary. Just stacking the rocks in a way so that gravity holds them in place and thus also holds the soil behind them in place makes a very attractive interior for the hillside aviary. Native rocks have another decided advantage also -- they're free.

Even if you are neither an amateur nor an accomplished rock worker, you can always use bricks to construct your terraces. Though bricks do not offer the character of native stone, they are reasonably cheap, readily available, and perfectly formed and uniform so that placing them as a straight or curved terracing material is quite simple. Bricks are available in a variety of colors, and some styles of bricks that are larger than the standard size are also manufactured for the construction industry. These larger bricks are available at any well-stocked building supply location. A perusal of what is available to you locally will allow you to choose a color and style that will complement the location of your aviary.

Aviary doors are important enough that they are covered in detail in Chapter 6. For the purposes of this discussion, I will only mention here the necessity of having doors that open easily and close with a small space on the top, bottom and sides. Though a door that sticks to the framing on one edge is no great problem in warmer climates, when you have a tight door in areas of freezing weather, you are asking for trouble. Freezing nights often follow a rainy weather front that may come through your area. This rain will do two things to the wood door and its framing. First, the wood will become damp and wet, and secondly, the wood will expand as it soaks up water. This combination will make a sticky door very tight indeed, and once the temperature goes below freezing, this door will freeze shut to the point that you will not be able to open it without tearing out the side of the aviary.

Should you have this happen, and before you cut a hole in the wire to get into the aviary, there is another way to get the door open. Fill a standard metal watering can with hot water, and gradually pour it around the door and its framing. This hot water will gradually thaw the frozen wood, but you may have to use more than one can of hot water. At any rate, within a few minutes, the door will be thawed enough to open. In order to prevent this from happening again, immediately use some tool to plane the door down to the point where it will swing freely, even when soaking wet. If you cannot maneuver a wood plane to do this, either a drawknife or hammer and wood chisel is sure to do the job adequately.

The most difficult type of aviary that I have ever attempted to build was a large, free-form aviary placed on a slope of about 30 degrees. None of the corners were square, and the upright posts were placed at varying distances from each other. This meant that the framing material had to be cut to different lengths, and no two pieces of the framing material were the same size. The wire that was placed over the framing also had to be cut to custom lengths and at custom angles for each section of the aviary. The result was attractive enough, but had taken far more time than should have been necessary for the construction and had resulted in greater than normal waste of material from cutting each piece to a custom fit. Should you decide to go with a free-form aviary, at least be sure that the widest area between two upright supports is no more than the width of the wire or hardware cloth that you will be using. This will make covering the framing much easier once you get that framing fastened in place and completed.

Acclimating any new finches or other small cage birds to your outdoor aviary conditions is often only a matter of controlling the microorganisms they are exposed to and feeding them a balanced diet that is high in complete protein, as well as all of the vital vitamins and minerals they need. These tiny birds have very limited body reserves when illness strikes, and for this reason, a sick finch almost invariably dies. Any harmful bacteria that they pick up can infect and shut down their digestive tracts, and these harmful microorganisms will result in the bird's death in short order. All new birds in the aviary must have time to develop their immunity to these harmful bacteria and other microorganisms.

You can give them the time they need to develop their immunity to unfamiliar microorganisms by treating their drinking water with about one drop of a common household sodium hypochlorite bleach to each three or four ounces of water. This will kill all of the harmful microorganisms in the water and in the digestive tract when the birds drink the water, without harming the birds in the least. Use this treatment for 3 days if some birds are sick, but only for one day as a preventative treatment. The chlorine will kill any bacteria or other microorganisms and give the birds a chance to develop an immunity to them. This immunity can be developed from just the presence of dead microorganisms very rapidly. After all, this is the way most human inoculations and vaccines work. Chlorine destroys vitamin E on contact however, so don't use any chlorine treatment on a constant basis.

I have found this simple treatment nearly 100% effective in preventing sickness in newly acquired birds. In cities where the water is already heavily chlorinated, this treatment may not be necessary. Taking finches for veterinary care, however, is simply never cost effective. The sick bird will be dead before any culture can be made or any effective antibiotic prescribed. Though many individuals in the past have ridiculed this chlorine treatment as at best useless and at worst dangerous to the birds, I feel sure that they haven't even tried this treatment for themselves on birds that were obviously ill. I have used it for many years, and stand solidly behind this recommendation for any new birds added to your collection. Despite the many aviculturists who are not in favor of this treatment, when you eliminate the emotions and cut down to the bottom line, it is this: the treatment works.

Another factor needs to be mentioned that will make catching birds in the outdoor aviary far easier. Young birds or extra pairs that you are moving to another aviary need to be caught up several times a year. The alcoves discussed in Chapter 6 are one means of doing this very effectively. If you have decided against having an alcove at your aviary entrance, you should leave one side of the aviary completely clear of any perches, feeders, nesting sites or plants. This will make the birds in the aviary much easier to catch as they fly along this clear side of the aviary. Anyone who has tried to catch birds that are flitting among perches, branches, nests and feeders will recognize quite readily the importance of leaving this one side of the aviary clear of all obstacles. The larger the aviary, the more important this cleared area becomes.

Before you place your nesting receptacles in the aviary, remember that the birds are most likely to accept a nesting site in an area that the birds consider to be hidden. After all, without a hidden nest, the bird would have no chance to raise young ones in the wild. A nest in plain sight would be an invitation to the first predator that came along to destroy it and eat the eggs or babies within the nest. Even with a hidden nest, this happens very frequently with wild birds. Remember that the smaller birds and their nests are prey to a large variety of mammals and reptiles. They are also preferred prey for many of the larger birds, such as the jays and raptors. In order to maintain the balance of nature and the balance of the species in nature, a pair of small birds needs to raise only two babies that live to reach adult breeding age and then begin breeding on their own. For every pair of small birds that manages to raise four youngsters to this stage, another pair will be killed and eaten, with no young raised.

In our aviaries, we protect and care for our birds so that the balance of nature is negated. We plan and expect for each pair that we keep to raise twenty, thirty, or even more young ones. When any predator comes upon this bounty of prey and food, it is only natural that they make a very serious attempt to thin out this overpopulation. In a natural situation, the limitation of food alone would prevent this concentration of birds in such a small area. When you look at your outdoor aviary from the eyes of the predators and the requirements of the balance of nature, it is easy to see why we wage a continual battle to protect the birds in our outdoor aviaries from their dangerous enemies.

As a final note, when you build an outdoor aviary of any type, even if it's only a growing pen for pheasant or quail chicks, be sure to make that pen or aviary large enough and tall enough that you can get into it and move around in it easily. You will need to refill feeders and waterers frequently, and eventually you will need to catch up the birds to transfer them to a larger permanent aviary. If the aviary is so low that you cannot move around in it while bending over, the top of the aviary is much too low, and will cause you unending problems. Never build an aviary that is more than 12 inches below your standing height, unless it is small enough that you can reach all corners of the aviary from the door. If you do build a low aviary that you have to crawl into, you will certainly suffer back strain at a minimum, along with unending frustration and disgust at yourself for failing to plan ahead a little better.

At one time, I built a small pen just three feet tall and four feet wide by eight feet long as a growing pen for young pheasants. After using this for some time, I came to the conclusion that the wire and framing material that was saved in the construction of this low aviary was not worth the additional effort and frustration that was required to work with the birds in this low enclosure. In addition, there is always the later necessity to catch the birds for transfer to a more permanent and larger aviary. If you are building an aviary of this type, make it no less than one foot shorter than you are tall. In other words, if you are six feet tall, make the aviary at least five feet tall. This will allow you enough space to move within the aviary when you need to without being forced to crawl on your hands and knees.

Chapter 2

Wood Framing
for Aviary Construction

Wood is probably the most widely used construction material in the world. Though certain areas specialize in adobe or stone construction, most smaller buildings are constructed using wood framing. In cold, forested areas, people often build their homes and buildings from logs. Even the buildings of brick and concrete block construction use wood for most interior framing. In addition, wood is widely used in wall paneling, furniture, and in interior and exterior decoration. Though there are substitutes for wood, all of them are considerably more expense and more difficult to manufacture and obtain.

This chapter will cover the advantages and disadvantages of wood for use in aviary framing in detail. However, the advantages to the use of wood in your aviary framing far outweigh the disadvantages. For general use, wood framing is usually the most satisfactory material for constructing the aviary frame. Also, you can fasten the aviary wire or hardware cloth to wood framing more easily and cheaply than is possible with any other type of aviary framing. Chapter 3 covers alternate materials that you can use for aviary framing.

For aviary construction, wood is by far the easiest to find and most commonly available framing material. Wood is an easy material to work with and requires only basic carpentry tools for the necessary shaping and cutting. Anyone can fasten wood framing together easily with the nails, nuts and bolts, screws or prefabricated metal fasteners that are available in any hardware store or home improvement center. Wood framing is also by far the cheapest method of aviary construction. All other framing options will cost considerably more, and will also have other disadvantages.

Wood also has its disadvantages, of course. First and most obvious, wood will be sure to rot in time. Wood that is exposed to dampness and to the bacteria of the soil rots very rapidly. Within a year or two, the soil's microorganisms will reduce a piece of wood to a soft, spongy mass that the larger earthworms and insects can use

23

for food. In this way, wood is broken down into its basic elements and returned to the soil. The rotting of a piece of wood will begin at any point where the wood remains damp enough to begin the growth and multiplication of the bacteria that perform this function in nature.

Even when you can protect wood from dampness and weather influences, dry rot can occur, again caused by a variety of microorganisms whose sole function is to transform wood to its constituent elements and return it to the soil. Dry rot is exactly what the name implies; wet wood is not necessary to start this process, and the microorganisms that perform this function get all of the moisture they need from the air itself.

Dry rot is vital in nature to begin the breakdown of standing dead trees and other woody plants. Though these microorganisms are often a disaster in our homes and buildings, they are also vital in the greater scheme of things for the breakdown of the wood in dead trees and fallen limbs into their basic constituents and elements and returning them to the soil for reuse. Nature's recycling through the use of these microscopic life forms is a marvel to behold, though it causes us unending problems in our homes and buildings.

Termites are another hazard that you must consider when making any aviary framing out of wood. Some of the wood used in aviary framing must be near the ground or in direct contact with the soil, and termites have a marvelous way of finding the wood that they need for their food and their existence. Even if the wood is up on a concrete foundation, the termites are perfectly capable of building a safe tunnel over the concrete to get to the wood above. This is a common occurrence, and huge industries have been built from the need to exclude these termites from our wooden homes and buildings.

A number of different types of wood are cut and made into lumber and are easily found at any lumber yard in any city or town in the U. S. or Canada. Any wood that is suitable for house construction will also be suitable for the construction of an aviary. Fir, spruce and pine are three of the woods that are in common use in various parts of the United States and Canada for construction. Hemlock is less common, as it tends to splinter easily. Any lumber yard in any city or town can supply wood that is suitable for aviary framing in a variety of standard lengths. Most home improvement locations will also precut the lumber for you to nearly any size you might need for the framing of an aviary.

This discussion will cover two general types of wood that are likely to be found and used in framing an aviary. The first type of wood is the regular, standard precut kiln-dried lumber, and it is probably the cheapest type of wood available for framing an aviary. This lumber is available anywhere at a reasonable price, as wood is one of our most commonly used and most useful building materials. Fortunately, wood is also a renewable resource. With any amount of foresight and planning, there will always be enough wood available for our use in building and construction.

Two inch by two inch lumber, written as 2 X 2, and usually called "2 by 2's", is available, and it is suitable for the framing of small aviaries. However, this size is more difficult to work with than the standard size of 2 inch by 4 inch lumber, written as 2 X 4 and called "2 by 4's", especially when you are trying to fasten the corners of an aviary. Still, with a normal amount of care in fastening the wood of the frame together, the 2 inch by 2 inch lumber is probably the best for a small aviary. Don't expect it to be cheaper than the standard 2" X 4" lumber, however. For every piece of 2 X 2 sold, there are many hundreds of 2 X 4's sold. This economy of scale means that the 2 X 2 lumber may even be more expensive than the 2 X 4's. Also, be aware that the size designation is applied before the wood is planed to a smooth surface. The actual size is about 1 ½ inches by 1 ½ inches.

The 2" by 4" lumber comes in a standard wall framing size, and builders commonly refer to this size as a "2 by 4 stud". This size is a pre-cut, standard size for use in wall framing, and many millions of them are cut and kiln dried every year. As a result of the huge amount of manufacturing and marketing of this lumber size, it will be the cheapest size for you to buy and use in your aviary framing. If you plan to use kiln-dried wood for your aviary framing, plan your aviary to use this size of lumber everywhere possible, since it will be the cheapest size available. Again, the size measurement applies to the lumber before planing. The actual size of the finished wood is about 1 ½ inches by 3 ½ inches.

The second basic type of wood that you will want to consider is pressure-treated lumber. This type of lumber is treated with a preservative, usually an arsenic compound, to prevent the growth of microorganisms, and to repel and kill insects, as well. Most pressure-treated lumber has a greenish color because of the preservative that has soaked into the lumber. Pressure-treated lumber is also considerably more expensive than the standard kiln-dried lumber.

However, for outdoor use, the pressure-treated lumber is far superior to the kiln-dried lumber, which is manufactured and sold primarily for interior use. Even in contact with the soil as the base of an aviary wall, the pressure-treated lumber will last for many years. It will actually crack, split and decompose more rapidly when exposed to the air and used as the side or top framing for the aviary. This is because the drying action of the sun and wind neutralizes the preservatives more rapidly than occurs with the portions of the framing that are in contact with the soil and remain damp.

Pressure-treated lumber is available in a variety of standard lengths, beginning with lengths of eight feet. As the pressure-treatment chemicals used on this wood are toxic to microorganisms and termites, they can also be toxic to you. Always wear gloves when handling the pressure-treated lumber, as the toxic arsenic compounds can be absorbed through your skin. Though handling a few pressure-treated 2 X 4's for a couple of days while building your aviary is unlikely to cause you to absorb enough of the toxic compounds to result in sickness, handling them constantly without hand protection, day in and day out, should be avoided. Any toxic compound of this type has a cumulative effect, so use your common sense and a reasonable amount of protection, and you should never experience any problem caused by handling the pressure-treated lumber.

If you decide to go with wooden framing for your outdoor aviary, from my personal experience, I now always recommend using this pressure-treated lumber. It is somewhat more difficult to work with, but the danger of insect and rot damage is eliminated for the first years of aviary use. I have checked pressure-treated lumber that was used as a base for my own aviaries and was in contact with the ground for a period of nine years. This lumber still showed no signs of rot or insect damage.

Once you have decided on wood framing for your aviary and the type of wood you want to use, the next step is purchasing the material you will need for the construction of your aviary. Any building supply store or home improvement center will carry the wood framing material you need in stock. If you live in an area of small population, there may only be one location that sells this material anywhere near you.

However, if you live in a population center that serves a million or more people, there will be a large number of outlets that will carry lumber. In this case, it will pay you to check around and see which outlet has material of the best quality, and at the same time, material of the best price. The large, national home improvement centers do not always have either the best quality nor the best price, though at times you can find identical items at the large chain stores that are considerably cheaper than the same items available at any other store in the area. It does pay to shop around, particularly when you are in a new area and have a considerable building project ahead of you in the construction of a variety of aviaries for all of the birds you want to keep.

Should you decide to go with pressure-treated wood, as mentioned before, you should be aware that working with it is more difficult than working with the standard kiln-dried lumber. First, pressure-treated lumber is wet. This means that it is more difficult to cut and drill than is kiln-dried lumber. This wetness also is your warning that the wood cells have stretched about as far as they will stretch to accommodate the preservative treatment liquid. For most methods of fastening the lumber together for your aviary framing, this means that you must drill what is called a pilot hole before inserting the nail, screw, or other fastener. Failing to do this will cause the wood to stretch beyond its limits, and it will split. Nothing is more exasperating than to have the end of a very carefully cut and sized piece of aviary framing split when you attempt to fasten it to the other aviary framing. Drilling a pilot hole beforehand will solve this problem and will end up giving you a much more solid and more durable aviary frame.

When using the pressure-treated lumber for aviary framing, most aviculturists will fasten the hardware cloth or other wire on the outside of the framing material. This is fine for any of the finches, doves, quail or softbills that will not chew on the wood of the framing. However, should you ever contemplate putting any psittacine birds in the aviary, this will be unsatisfactory. Any of the small or large parrots will chew on wood instinctively, and in chewing on the pressure-treated wood, they can get an excess of arsenic from the treated wood and consequently die of arsenic poisoning. The simplest means of providing safety from this for your psittacine birds is to place your hardware cloth on the *inside* of the aviary framing, rather than on the outside, as you would normally do. When fastened on the inside, you can easily place the wire so that the metal covers all of the pressure treated wood. I have used aviaries constructed in this manner for a variety of parrot-type birds, including cockatiels, quaker parakeets, budgies and lovebirds, and have never subsequently encountered any problem from the pressure-treated wood.

Most wood that is not earmarked for furniture construction, cabinet work, and finish carpentry will have knots. A knot marks the place on the tree trunk that the piece of lumber was cut from where a limb was growing out of the trunk. The wood that forms a knot is much harder than the other areas of the piece of wood. A knot is much harder to nail than the softer parts of the wood, and it can also indicate a dangerously brittle and weak spot in the piece of lumber with which you are working. The types of wood used for pressure-treated lumber are particularly noted for having very hard and brittle knots. The best lumber does not go through the pressure-treatment process. As you cut your lumber to the correct size for use in your aviary, be aware of the knots, and try to make your cuts so that the area where you must fasten the piece of wood does not contain a knot. Being aware of this potential problem will take you about ninety percent of the way to preventing it from causing you any problems as you construct the framing of your aviary.

When you are purchasing the wood framing material that you feel you will need for your new aviary, at the same time you should be considering what method you will use to fasten the wood framing together. At least four basic methods are available for fastening this framing securely and permanently. Each offers advantages and disadvantages that you should be aware of before deciding which method you will use in the construction of your aviary frame. These four primary fastening methods are fastening with nails, using screws to fasten the framing, using bolts and nuts to join the framing pieces, or using standard prefabricated metal brackets to fasten the framing together. At times, a combination of two or more of these methods will give you a much better and more durable frame for the finished aviary.

Nailing has the decided advantage of being the cheapest method of fastening two pieces of wood together while at the same time being a very secure and permanent method of fastening them. Using the standard sixteen penny (usually written 16d) common nails is possible, but these nails have no rust protection, and outside exposure to the wind and rain will cause them to begin rusting rather rapidly. Rust streaks on the wood framing of your aviary are unsightly at best, and the rust will bleed through most paints and will virtually scream "stupid amateur!" to anyone who is familiar with construction and knows how to use construction materials to the best advantage. At worst, rusty nails weaken the original strength of the framing construction over a period of time to the point where the framing will not hold together under a fierce wind or storm.

For outside construction, hot galvanized common nails are available that have a coating of zinc which prevents the nail from rusting. These nails are a little more expensive than standard common nails, but for outdoor aviary construction, they are well worth the added expense. As the liquid zinc does not adhere to the nail smoothly and evenly, the rough outside coating of the nail holds it in the wood nearly as effectively as a screw would hold it. Pulling a misnailed piece of framing off of the aviary is not an easy job when it has been nailed with a galvanized nail. Once you do get it loose, the nail will probably be bent, and the galvanizing coating will be cracked away from sections of the nail. If this is the case, discard the nail, or use it for an indoor application. To reuse a nail with broken and chipped galvanizing is to ask for it to rust and fail to do the best job possible on your aviary.

Another type of nail is available which is electro-galvanized. This bonds a very fine coat of zinc to the nail, which leaves the nail perfectly smooth and shiny. These nails are better than the standard steel common nails, but not much better. They will not last nearly as long as the hot galvanized nails.

For nailing lumber that is to be outdoors under all temperature and weather conditions, I always recommend using the hot galvanized nails. To prevent splitting from excessively stretched wood cells, or the presence of a knot in the wood, you should always drill a pilot hole that is nearly as large as the shaft of the nail for at least three-quarters of the length of that nail. Once this hole is drilled, you can easily hammer the nail into the two pieces of wood, and it will hold completely securely without splitting the wood as it goes in. Though the joining of wood framing pieces is not always possible with nails alone, this is by far the best and cheapest method of fastening the wood framing for an outdoor aviary.

Screws are a second method that is available to fasten the wood framing pieces in place. Though most screws are made for interior use, you can purchase stainless steel screws at any large hardware store or home improvement center. Stainless steel is impervious to rusting and corrosion. However, the stainless steel screws are far more expensive, at least four times the cost of the standard metal screws of the same size. Nevertheless, for those aviary applications when a screw seems to be the best method for fastening two pieces of framing together, stainless steel screws are available for outside use as a permanent, corrosion-proof method for fastening pieces of your aviary wood framing.

Again, when you are using screws for fastening, a pilot hole is absolutely necessary for each screw before it is screwed into the wood. Failure to drill a pilot hole that is nearly as wide as the shaft of the screw will make placing the screw into the wood impossibly difficult. Also, without the pilot hole, you are likely to split the wood, thus destroying its ability to support the weight of the aviary and the wire mesh covering of the aviary.

The third method for fastening wood framing for an aviary is by using bolts, along with nuts and possibly also washers. A variety of types of bolts are available on the market that will be usable outdoors. In addition, stainless steel nuts and bolts are also available at a considerably higher price which will be corrosion-proof over any length of time they are in use in the outdoor aviary. A hole must be drilled in the wood to accommodate the bolt, and if the head of the bolt and the nut are not wide enough, you will also have to use a washer under the head of the bolt and under the nut at the other end when using this method for fastening the framing of an aviary. Though bolts and nuts are a solid and stable method for fastening aviary framing, they have limited usefulness, and they are the least effective method for fastening the framing for an outdoor aviary.

The last of the common methods for fastening wood framing are the preformed metal bracing and joining pieces that come in a wide variety of sizes and shapes. The

The last of the common methods for fastening wood framing are the preformed metal bracing and joining pieces that come in a wide variety of sizes and shapes. The most useful for most aviary applications are the simple L-shaped corner braces, and the flat metal joining pieces for fastening framing on a single plane. Each of these types of metal braces is predrilled with holes to accommodate small nails for fastening them to the wood. When you are working with any two-inch lumber, the 1½ inch hot galvanized roofing nails are best for fastening these metal braces to the wood framing. For these small nails, no pilot holes are necessary. Also, they will not penetrate through the 2-inch lumber, so you can easily nail them on both sides of the framing member to hold it doubly secure. These pre-drilled metal pieces have a variety of uses when framing an outdoor aviary, and they are particularly valuable for fastening framework when you are using angles other than the standard square corners of 90 degrees.

You are not ready to begin the framing construction of your aviary until you have decided which type of aviary wire or hardware cloth you will be using in the construction of your aviary. If the aviary wire is 36 inches wide, you will want to be sure that your framing material is placed about two inches less than 36 inches apart, so that you will have room to fasten it along both edges. If the aviary wire is 48 inches wide, you will need spacing of about 46 inches between each framing member. The smaller the mesh on the aviary wire or hardware cloth, the less space you will need for fastening. With ¼-inch mesh hardware cloth, leaving half an inch of framing for nailing or stapling on each side will be sufficient. With ½-inch mesh, you should leave at least ¾ of an inch of nailing or stapling space. Refer to Chapter 4 for detailed information on the aviary wiring types that are available and how to fasten them securely and permanently.

While you only need to consider the size of the wire when framing the sides of the aviary, the top and any other covered portions of the aviary need a great deal more thought and planning. The types of material and the slope you can use for the top and roof of the aviary have been covered in Chapter 1. However, the framing is even more crucial to the design of the top of the aviary. In mild climates where snow is limited to a few flurries only a couple of times a year or with no chance of snow at all, your only considerations need be the ability of the aviary to shed water and to withstand wind.

For protection from rain and wind, you can plan the framing solely with the size of the wire, hardware cloth, or roofing material as factors in the spacing of the framing. Measure your material for the top of the aviary and any protected sides carefully, however, to allow space for nailing or stapling, and don't neglect to take into consideration the overlap that is necessary for the installation of the fiberglass or polycarbonate roofing material.

When you live in an area where snow is expected every winter, the framing of the top of the aviary will have to be much sturdier than what is necessary in the milder climate zones. The covered areas of the aviary will, of course, require the sturdier framing. Place your support framing at the spacings recommended below to provide the best support for the roofing material when it becomes covered with a heavy layer of snow during the winter.

Also, however, don't forget that snow will accumulate on the wire top of the aviary, so the framing of that portion also must be capable of bearing the additional weight of a heavy snowfall. Quarter-inch mesh hardware cloth will catch nearly all of the snow and will hold it either until you brush it off of the aviary top, or until it melts. Half-inch mesh hardware cloth will also catch most of the snow and will hold it on top of the aviary. Surprisingly, even one-inch mesh chicken wire will catch and hold about 90 percent of the snow that accumulates in an average snowfall.

I cannot overstress the importance of paying attention to this need for snowfall protection for the top of your aviary, if you live in a climate area where heavy snowfalls are expected each winter. If you do not pay attention to this framing need during the initial construction of the top and roof of your aviary, you will have a great deal of trouble dealing with it later, after the snows begin to fall in the winter.

For areas that receive appreciable amounts of snow, your main framing pieces for the top of the aviary should be no farther than 24 inches apart. Also, a cross member should be fastened at least every four feet between each of the main framing members. Fastening a cross member every two feet would be far more effective. This will make solid fastening of your roofing material much easier, and it will make the top of the aviary solid enough and stable enough to remain unaffected by a heavy snowfall.

Finally, a complete coverage of the subject of winter snowfall preparation requires that I stress the importance of the upright supports of your aviary. A roof or top of the aviary that will support all of the heavy snow that you might expect is no guarantee that the upright supports will be strong enough to support the additional weight of several feet of snow on the top of the aviary. During your initial work and construction, make sure that your upright supports for the walls of the aviary are as stable and as well braced as you can make them. If this strength is lacking in the walls and sides of the aviary, these upright supports will not be able to hold the weight of a heavy snowfall without collapsing and causing the loss of your birds.

As a final note on the use of wood for aviary framing, be sure to stop and think before you begin your purchase of wood framing materials or begin the actual construction of the aviary framing. Consider all of the factors that may affect the aviary in its final form, everything from the location and exposure of the aviary to the local normal range of weather conditions and the possibility and frequency of extreme weather conditions. You will need to consider each of these factors carefully, as they will all have a bearing on the ultimate framing and usefulness of the aviary.

Chapter 3

Alternate Framing for Aviary Construction

Though most alternate forms of aviary framing make use of metals, certain kinds of plastic can also serve this function. Each of the types of alternate materials that can be used for aviary framing will be discussed in some detail in this chapter. Each type of possible framing material that you might use, of course, will have both advantages and disadvantages for use in the framing of an aviary.

Metals are the most permanent method of aviary frame construction available, and any aviary framework constructed of metal will far outlast the wood construction methods discussed in the last chapter. Three metals or alloys are normally used for framing that makes use of the 'angle iron' style of metal fabrication. The cheapest is iron alloyed with other metals to make steel. In a medium price range for the metals is aluminum. The most expensive, hardest, and most durable metallic alloy for aviary construction is stainless steel. In addition, the possibility of using both the plastic and metal piping for the purpose of aviary framing will be covered in this chapter. Each of these possibilities and alternatives, their advantages and disadvantages, and their strengths and weaknesses will be discussed in detail in the following paragraphs.

As a beginning, it is necessary to state that the metals are by far the most expensive materials for the framing of an aviary. The cheapest of these metals when used for aviary framing will cost from three to ten times the amount of money that is required for the construction of a wood frame aviary. Aluminum framing material will be about double the price of steel framing. Stainless steel framing material is very difficult to locate, but it is quite expensive, and it will be several times the cost of standard steel framing.

Metals are not cheap, nor are they a renewable resource. Wood, by contrast, is both reasonably inexpensive, and it is a renewable resource. All of the metals are incomparably more difficult to mine, refine and manufacture than lumber of similar sizes, and this accounts for their relatively high cost for use in aviary construction.

31

Wood, by contrast, requires only cutting and drying to prepare it for its ultimate uses. The framing metals also vary considerably in pricing. For example, compare the retail cost of an aluminum cooking pan to the same size available in stainless steel. The cost will be roughly five times as much for the stainless steel.

Many relatively cheap sets of imported stainless steel cookware are available, but the quality of the stainless steel used in their manufacture is extremely poor. The alloys are the poorest quality available, and they are poorly mixed before forming into the cooking utensils. Within a very short time, rust spots will begin appearing on the cookware in spots where the iron has not bonded adequately with the other metals in the alloy, and those flaws will show up as rust spots when oxygen bonds with the free iron in the finished cookware.

Other types of metal pieces used for a variety of applications in the industrial sector may also be available for aviary framing. Special types of shelving and shelving supports are used in many industries, and if you have access to the materials used in that industry, be sure to consider their possible value for use in aviary framing. Be particularly aware that when styles and methods change, quite a large quantity of suitable framing material may become available at a very reasonable price. Also, stores that are closing often have a wide variety of used shelving material offered for sale at very reasonable prices that can be easily adapted for use in framing an aviary.

As an example, titanium and its alloys are very strong, light weight metals. Because of these characteristics, these metals are used widely in the aviation industry. When changes in aircraft styles and support occur, it may be possible to get pieces of titanium and titanium alloys that are no longer needed for aircraft use, but are quite well adaptable for aviary framing.

STEEL FRAMING

In proceeding on to a more detailed study of these metals, the least expensive metal for aviary framing will be steel. Preformed pieces of steel are available in a variety of sizes and shapes for use as framing for your aviary. Though flat pieces are available, they are a poor choice for aviary construction, as they are far too flexible to provide an adequate framework for an aviary. The pieces preformed at a 90 degree angle are the strongest and most durable, and you can find them in a variety of lengths and thicknesses to serve any purpose. Most hardware stores carry several different types in several different lengths, and will be happy to special order any type or length for you that they don't normally carry in stock, if it is available from their warehouse or from their supplier.

Collectively, these pieces of iron formed at a 90° angle are referred to as 'angle iron', though they are not formed from pure iron, but are a steel alloy. Pure iron is extremely brittle, and you will normally find it used only in such heat sensitive and non-movable uses as in the gratings in a fireplace. Steel is iron that has been mixed and alloyed with carbon and usually with other metals, such as manganese, chromium, nickel, molybdenum, copper, tungsten, cobalt, or silicon, depending upon the final characteristics that are needed for the strength and durability of the resulting product.

For aviary framing, angle iron is reasonably easy to work with, it is extremely strong and durable, and it is the commonest and cheapest metal available for aviary construction. There are a variety of types of angle iron, some of them solid, and some with holes and slots predrilled into them for attaching things like hardware cloth easily, without the necessity for drilling additional holes to fasten the wire. This predrilled angle iron is called 'slotted angle iron', and manufacturers fabricate it in varying thicknesses, strengths, and lengths, primarily for use as framing for the construction of shelving.

Slotted angle iron is available in a variety of sizes and patterns that will be able to suit any possible need. The difference in price between regular angle iron and slotted angle iron of the same size is usually minimal, but the saving in your time and effort through using the slotted angle iron will be huge. Custom drilling the holes in angle iron for your aviary will be a very slow and time-consuming job. In addition, as was previously mentioned, angle iron will cost you many times the amount that wood framing of a similar size would cost in the construction of your aviary.

If you don't like the idea of all of those unused holes in the slotted angle iron of your finished aviary, you can use the solid angle iron and only drill the holes where you need them. An electric drill will be a necessity, and a drill bit that is slightly larger than the diameter of the bolts that you will use to fasten the hardware cloth or wire. Even with the right drill and bit, drilling a hole in steel is not an easy job, and the need to drill at least ten of these holes in each piece of angle iron should make anyone pause to contemplate if this customizing is really worth all of the time and effort it requires, particularly when the slotted angle iron is usually available at a similar or even a lesser price.

When you use the slotted angle iron that is readily available in most large hardware stores and steel supply outlets, you will save yourself a huge amount of work in designing, measuring, and drilling holes. This pre-formed slotted angle iron has holes pre-drilled every half-inch or so, and at any conceivable spot where you may want to fasten the hardware cloth or any other item. When you use this type of framing, once the framing construction is completed, all you will then need to do is to fasten the wire onto the framing.

Once you have the holes in the angle iron, either prepunched or the ones that you've drilled yourself, and have your framing assembled in the final form of the aviary and in place, you are ready to attach the hardware cloth or wire to the framing. An easy way to do this is to use steel wire to run through the holes in the framing and the hardware cloth, twisting the piece of wire around the framing to hold the hardware cloth securely in place. This is fast and sturdy, but has several definite disadvantages.

The first disadvantage is the poor appearance of twisted wires all over the outside of the aviary. These wire ends sticking out, even when flattened as much as possible for the sake of appearance, will constantly snag clothing as you work around the finished aviary. Any pet rubbing against this wire will also snag its fur and will lose a little that will remain hanging on the aviary. For a construction method that is this expensive, twisted wires will give you a rather sloppy final appearance.

The second major disadvantage is far worse, for each one of those twisted pieces of wire offers a perfect spot for a bird to get a toe or a toenail caught and jammed tight. The bird will struggle to escape, and the least damage it will do is to tear off a toenail. More likely, you will find the bird hanging exhausted with a broken leg and the foot hanging by only a tendon. This will necessitate an amputation if you hope to save the bird's life, and this will be a disaster for a breeding male. Only one male who had lost a leg was still able to fertilize the hen in all of my past experience with breeding birds. Unfortunately, as you surely already know, if you leave any place in an aviary where a bird can catch a toe or a foot and mangle its leg, it is as sure as the sun rises that sooner or later a bird will do exactly that.

The third major disadvantage of using pieces of wire to fasten the hardware cloth to the framing is the possibility of rusting. Unless you use a type of stainless steel wire for fastening the hardware cloth, the wire will rust through in a surprisingly short time. Sunlight, water, wind and bird droppings will all hasten the joining of the oxygen in the air to any steel wire you use on the aviary to form rust.

The neatest method for fastening wire or hardware cloth to your steel aviary frame is through the use of short bolts, washers, and nuts to fasten the hardware cloth to the frame and to tighten it down. Depending on the size of the wire or hardware cloth you use, you may not have to use washers at all. The most economical and easily available size are the ½ inch hex nuts and bolts that are available at any hardware store. As you will need hundreds of these, it is wise to check around at the various stores in your area to see where they are available in boxes of 100 at the most reasonable price. Even within the same hardware chain, the price from one location to another may vary from $3.00 per hundred to over $5.00 per hundred. If you are building a large aviary or a bank of several joined aviaries, you will use many hundreds of nuts and bolts, and this difference in price will multiply into quite a number of dollars.

Another thing to keep in mind is that these standard nuts and bolts will rust in time. Particularly in areas where the birds splash water constantly and where the droppings accumulate, the bolts and nuts will rust rather rapidly. After a year or two, you may have a very difficult time removing these rusted bolts when you need to dismantle or move the cage or aviary.

For this reason, on any aviary that will be exposed to the full range of weather conditions, as well as to the splashing water and droppings of the birds, I would not hesitate to recommend that you use stainless steel nuts and bolts for the construction of your metal framed outdoor aviaries. Though these stainless steel fasteners will cost about three times as much as standard steel fasteners, they are easily available in any well-stocked hardware outlet, and they are well worth the additional expense.

This method of construction with angle iron, hardware cloth and bolts will be very secure, and nothing that is able to harm the birds, their eggs, or offspring will be able to gain access to the aviary between the wiring and the angle iron. Nothing short of major disaster, such as a major earthquake, tornado, or a vehicle or boulder plowing into the aviary, will be able to tear the hardware cloth or wire from the metal framing when it is fastened in this manner. Short bolts with the accompanying nuts and washers of the correct size will be more expensive than fastening with wire, of course, but the end result will be far more esthetically pleasing and far more permanent than will the use of pieces of twisted wire to fasten the hardware cloth onto the finished framing for the aviary.

The main disadvantage to the use of steel for aviary framing is the natural rusting that will take place over a period of time unless you treat the metal with a protective coating to exclude the oxygen in the air and prevent the resulting joining with the steel angle iron to form rust. Steel is not rustproof, though it will take many years for the rusting to work its way through a piece of slotted angle iron. Still, with minimal rust protection, you can count on the life of this slotted angle iron to be thirty years or more. Wood framing will not last nearly so long without constant attention.

There are a variety of coatings you can use to prevent the formation of rust on your angle iron framing. All of these coatings will have to be reapplied periodically, as nothing is surer than the corrosive effects of sun, wind, weather and bird droppings. Still, they may be worthwhile if you intend this aviary to be available for use over the longest term.

There are many types of spray paint and rust-inhibitive coatings on the market. If you decide to use one of them, check out what is available, and its possible effect on any birds you intend to keep in the aviary. Though doves and most softbills will not chew on the wire or the protective coating, such birds as budgerigars, cockatiels and parrots certainly will! Using anything to coat the wire that might be toxic to the birds will not be wise. You never know how your interests may change in the future and what different species you may want to house in the aviary many years down the road.

Another decided disadvantage to the use of steel framing is the weight of the finished product. Though this is an advantage during high winds, should you ever need to move the aviary over a few feet or to disassemble it for a longer distance move and more permanent relocation, you will find that you are dealing with several hundred pounds of dead weight, certainly more than one person can easily handle.

I discovered this disadvantage even in building a bank of breeding cages out of slotted angle iron. Though the finished bank of cages was very solid and permanent, it was also so heavy that I could not lift it alone. Anything that you cannot handle alone is likely to cause you problems in the future. The weight of cages or aviaries built out of angle iron may in time become a liability and a decided disadvantage.

As a final note on the use of angle iron, be aware that there are a number of manufacturers of this type of material. Each makes the material slightly differently, and the holes may be drilled in the slotted angle iron in slightly different locations. As a result, the materials from different manufacturers are NOT interchangeable for the construction of your cages and aviaries. Be certain that all of your framing material comes from the same location, or at least from the same manufacturer. The use of materials from more than one source will almost certainly cause you problems in matching the pre-drilled holes for the framing construction.

ALUMINUM FRAMING

Aluminum has its owns set of advantages and disadvantages when used as a construction material in aviary construction. Chief among its advantages is the very light weight of aluminum and its ready availability. Most hardware stores and home improvement centers now carry a range of standard sizes and strengths available in pieces of angled aluminum. Cages or aviaries constructed with aluminum framing will never be too heavy to work with comfortably, and they will be more long-lasting than a comparable aviary built out of wood. Incidentally, in Britain and in some other English-speaking areas, this word is spelled a-l-u-m-i-n-i-u-m, and it is pronounced al-yu-mín-i-um.

Aluminum is also soft enough that you can easily drill holes in it for use in fastening the aviary wire or hardware cloth to the framing. This is fortunate, for aluminum pieces do not come in the standard slotted format so common in steel angle iron. Also, a hack saw can be used without undue effort to cut pieces of angle aluminum to any exact length that you might need. If you take care to use a sharp blade and a solid, immovable cutting surface, your cuts will be quite exact and will appear very neat. Aluminum is a very common metal and a very easy metal to work with, and this accounts for much of its current popularity for a variety of uses. We are fortunate to live in a time when electricity is so abundant for the refining and smelting of aluminum for our needs.

When purchasing pieces of pre-formed aluminum angle, you will find that the cost is from 50% more to about double the price of a comparable piece of angle iron. Thus, an aviary with aluminum framing will cost considerably more than an aviary with angle iron framing. Again I do not recommend using the flat pieces of aluminum anywhere on the aviary framing, as it is far too flexible to have any framing value.

Nothing is perfect, however, and aluminum does have its disadvantages. The price has already been mentioned as a disadvantage. Also, in time, aluminum will oxidize when exposed for long periods to the sun, wind and weather. This oxidation takes the form of a soft, whitish coating on the surface of any object made from aluminum.

The worst disadvantage of aluminum for aviary construction is the fact that it is very susceptible to corrosion from alkalis. As the birds' droppings are alkaline in nature, any dropping that adheres to a piece of aluminum framing in an aviary will eat away a small part of the aluminum framing. This will take the form of actual pits in the aluminum in an aviary frame. Over a period of time, and in a location where the birds frequently leave their droppings, this can become very unsightly. Though it is doubtful that any combination of droppings over a number of years would eat away the aluminum framing to the point that it would no longer act as a support for the aviary, the appearance would continue to deteriorate over the years.

Many aviaries have been built using aluminum framing over the years, however, and most have been sturdy and attractive over the long term. The most impressive aviary that I have seen outside of a zoological park was constructed using aluminum framing, and the effect was quite pleasing. This aviary was 30 feet wide by 60 feet long, and about 12 feet tall, large enough for any avian species you could possibly want to put in it.

There are two basic methods for fastening the aluminum framing together and then fastening the hardware cloth or aviary wire to it. Either method makes a secure, long-lasting aviary, and all things considered, the cost of either method would probably be about the same.

The first method of fastening is to use nuts and bolts, as you would do for an aviary with a framing of angle iron. You will have to drill the holes in the aluminum framing, then fasten the wire or hardware cloth to this framing using a bolt, nut, and washers if necessary. Again, the use of stainless steel nuts and bolts, despite their added expense, is often a very worthwhile expenditure in the construction of an outdoor aviary framed in aluminum.

If you are using very small mesh hardware cloth, one-quarter inch or less, washers will not be necessary. For any mesh larger than one-quarter inch, washers to keep the wire tight and secure are always recommended. The standard, steel nuts and bolts will do the job, but they do have the disadvantage of rusting over a period of time when exposed to water and to the corrosive effect of the birds' droppings. Should you decide to use bolts with nuts to fasten the aluminum framing and then for attaching the hardware cloth, for the long-term beauty of an aluminum aviary, I would recommend using the stainless steel bolts and nuts for these fastening purposes. Though the stainless steel nuts and bolts are far more expensive, they are also permanent, reusable, and they will not corrode.

The second method for fastening aluminum framing and then fastening the hardware cloth to it is through the use of aluminum rivets. These rivets and the rivet gun to lock them in place are sold wherever a variety of sizes of aluminum are available, and in any well stocked hardware that carries a wide variety of tools. In order to fasten aluminum pieces with this method, you must first drill a hole for the rivet, then insert the rivet itself using the riveting gun. Once you become familiar with this riveting procedure, it goes quite rapidly. The final effect of this method of rivet fastening is also very neat and quite attractive.

As a final note on aluminum, as you visit the hardware stores and the home improvement centers in your area, you will note that many carry pieces of aluminum that are longer than six feet. Though this seems to be the maximum length for the slotted angle iron in all the hardware areas visited, aluminum is frequently available in lengths of eight, ten, or even twelve feet. When you can use these longer aluminum pieces, framing the longer dimensions of a large aviary becomes much easier.

STAINLESS STEEL FRAMING

Stainless steel angle iron is the third possible method that may be used for constructing the framing of an outdoor aviary. The great advantage of stainless steel is that this material is virtually indestructible. An aviary frame made out of stainless steel will last longer than your lifetime, but the wire or hardware cloth that you place around this framing to enclose the aviary will have to be replaced whenever it begins to rust. The greatest disadvantage to stainless steel framing will be the extremely high cost of this material. Stainless steel wire and hardware cloth are also available for this type of application, but it will also be quite hard to find and very expensive.

No hardware chain or outlet carries this stainless steel framing material as a stock item. Stainless steel angle iron is difficult to find, and you may have to go to a specialty supplier that deals only in the various types of steel and stainless steel framing materials that are used in the construction industry. Finding such a dealer may not be difficult in a large population area, but it will be nearly impossible if you live in a rural or relatively isolated area of low population density.

The style of stainless steel you will need for aviary framing is the slotted angle iron style. Stainless steel is extremely hard and difficult to drill holes in, so you will save a huge amount of work, effort and expense by purchasing the pre-drilled types. These will be easy to work with, and you can handle them in the same manner as you work with the standard slotted angle iron.

As already mentioned, stainless steel angle iron is not cheap. Stainless steel probably will be the most expensive type of material that you can use for aviary framing. While the standard slotted angle iron will cost you around $1.75 per foot at today's prices, the same size in stainless steel will cost several times this much. You will need to think long and hard to be certain that the cost of stainless steel is worthwhile for the applications for which you are using this material.

Also, cutting pieces to fit for entrances and other applications may have to be done where you purchase the standard lengths. Stainless steel is very difficult to cut, and unless you have your own metal shop and are familiar with all metals and their characteristics, you will be far better off having a professional shop do the cutting for you. The nominal charge for this service will be more than offset by the savings in time, work and the frustration of trying to cut this material yourself.

Once you have found a supplier for the stainless steel and have decided to use it for your aviary framing, by all means use the stainless steel bolts and nuts in your construction of the aviary with this type of framing. Unlike the hard to find framing pieces, the stainless steel bolts and nuts are available at any well stocked hardware store. It makes no sense to spend the large amount necessary for the stainless steel framing and then to fasten it together with the cheaper, regular steel nuts and bolts.

Also, anyone who is willing to go to the expense of stainless steel framing and fasteners should also put in the additional effort required to find and purchase the stainless steel hardware cloth. You will often find this type of hardware cloth used in laboratories and research organizations, as it is so much more easily cleaned and disinfected than are the standard steel or galvanized steel materials. The best place to search for this item is through a laboratory supply firm. The cost of a roll of this stainless steel hardware cloth will be several times the cost of a roll of standard galvanized steel hardware cloth.

PLASTIC FRAMING MATERIALS

The fourth alternate framing possibility for your aviary are the various types of stiff plastic pipe that are available on the market. These are not difficult to locate, and are usually fairly inexpensive. Large hardware and home improvement centers will carry at least one type of this pipe and the fittings that you can adapt for use in fastening the corners when you use this for aviary framing. Though the piping itself is fairly inexpensive, the fittings that are manufactured for fastening two pipes together may be far more expensive.

Another possible source for these plastic framing materials are the various outlets that carry the plastic materials for framing greenhouses, carports and other outdoor shelters. These outlets will also carry a variety of fittings for fastening the pieces of straight piping together. As these types of piping do not have to be safe for water and stable for water pressure, they may be less expensive that the types of pipe that serve the plumbing industry.

The primary disadvantage to the plastic piping is that most types of plastics become brittle and will crack and crumble when exposed to sunlight and outdoor weather conditions. Also, the PVC type of water pipe will become brittle with age and any blow may then shatter it. Before you invest in any type of plastic pipe for your aviary framing, be sure to check on the characteristics of the plastic, and ascertain to your own satisfaction that the pipe will last for the required number of years when used in your aviary.

A second disadvantage found in the use of plastic pipe as aviary framing is the difficulty in fastening wire or hardware cloth to the plastic framing. You can use neither nails nor bolts for fastening the wire to this framing, though there are two other methods of fastening that will work quite well for this plastic framing.

The first fastening method requires that you use short wires to tie the aviary netting onto the plastic framing. You can pre-cut the lengths of wire at a size that will allow you to thread it through the hardware cloth on one side and around the plastic pipe. Then, use a pair of pliers to twist the wire tight and to flatten the twisted portion so that it is of no danger to the birds. Actually, when fastening wire by this method, it is much better to twist the wire on the outside of the aviary to tighten it. This will eliminate most of the possibilities for a bird to get its toes caught in the wire

A second method of fastening is by using short screws with washers to hold the aviary wire on. You can accomplish this by drilling a small pilot hole in the plastic pipe where the screw is to attach. As the screw goes into the softer plastic, it will thread its own hole to hold the wire onto the pipe tightly and securely.

METAL PIPE FRAMING

You have a fifth possibility for an alternate type of aviary framing through the use of galvanized metal pipe. Those who raise the large psittacine birds often resort to the use of this type of framing, as these large parrots, cockatoos and macaws will be happy to chew on anything that is chewable.

In general, metal pipe is rather expensive. Because of this high cost of metal pipe, plumbers now often use the cheaper plastic pipe that is available. Particularly when you begin pricing galvanized metal pipe that is over one inch in diameter, you will likely decide that cheaper methods of aviary framing are sure to be much more economical and equally or even more satisfactory.

Neither are there a variety of methods for fastening wire or hardware cloth on the aviary framed with metal pipe. Using the piece of wire to fasten the hardware cloth to the framing, as discussed in the last section, is one method which will work satisfactorily. Also, you can drill holes in the metal pipe, then use machine screws with a washer to fasten the wire onto the metal framing.

The pipe and fencing that is made for chain link fencing applications is often the cheapest type of metal pipe framing that you can locate, primarily because manufacturers fabricate so much of this material that is sold at a far more reasonable price for use in fencing. Though the chain link fencing itself is overkill for most aviary applications, it is definitely needed and of value in aviaries that are designed for maintaining and breeding the large psittacine birds.

As a final note on alternate methods of framing, think for a while before you make a final decision on the framing material you will use. As noted in the first section of this chapter, the industrial sector uses a wide variety of materials for construction and shelving. Check around locally to see if any industry near you uses any special material that you may find useful as aviary framing. Often the ordering department of a company will be willing to place an order for you with their regular supplier. This is especially useful when the supplier may deal only in large quantities with established businesses.

Chapter 4

Hardware Cloth
And Other Wire

Once the framing is completed, the wire or hardware cloth that will be used to cover the framing can be attached. If you are building each section as a prefabricated panel, you can use a flat surface for attaching each piece of the wire to the framing. Though this construction method will require at least 25% more of the framing material, it has the distinct advantage of being easily taken apart for moving and reconstruction in a new area.

QUARTER-INCH MESH HARDWARE CLOTH

A wide variety of materials for covering the framing are available, but from sad experience, I can only recommend one type as completely safe, and that is the quarter-inch mesh hardware cloth. Anything larger will admit snakes or mice that can make your aviary a very dangerous place for your birds. This quarter-inch mesh hardware cloth is more expensive than the larger mesh sizes, but it is a small price to pay for the safety of your birds. Hardware cloth is available in most large hardware stores, and it is manufactured in rolls one hundred feet in length, and in varying widths from about 18 inches to 48 inches or four feet. The 36-inch and 48-inch width rolls are the easiest to find, and are usually also the most economical to purchase. Many hardware stores and home improvement centers carry short rolls, usually 25 feet in length, so you do not need to purchase more material than you need if you are building only a small aviary. The purchase of a hundred-foot roll, however, will get you the best price per foot for the quarter-inch mesh hardware cloth.

For outdoor aviary construction, the four foot widths are usually the most satisfactory, and for the amount of square feet contained in the roll, the four foot widths are also the most economical. Each individual piece of wire is welded where it joins every other piece, and this makes the whole section very sturdy and stable. At times in the manufacturing, an area of the wire will be crooked and uneven. Though this detracts from the appearance of the hardware cloth for its ultimate uses, these defects do not weaken the hardware cloth in any way. The welds are still completely stable and sturdy, and the wire will still serve its purpose on the aviary. No bird will ever be able to tear a hole in this type of hardware cloth, and as the finished product is galvanized, (covered with a thin coating of zinc), after the welding, it will last for many years without rusting.

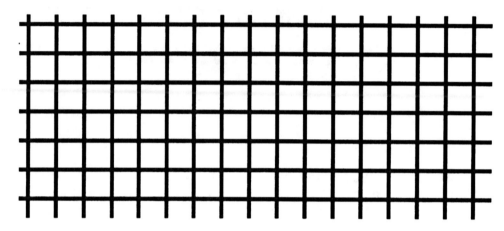

Illustration of 1/4 inch mesh hardware cloth

Cutting the hardware cloth can be very simple or very difficult, depending upon your available tools and the way you approach the cutting. Any type of wire cutters will accomplish the job of cutting the hardware cloth, but there is a much easier way. Especially when cutting many sections of the hardware cloth that is four feet wide, you need to buy a large pair of metal cutting snips, commonly called tinsnips. Any large hardware store carries them at a reasonable price, and these snips will make cutting the hardware cloth in a perfect, straight line simplicity itself. Though one of these cutters is certainly more expensive than the smaller ones, the hassles, frustration and grief that a pair of these will save you over the years are well worth the additional cost of the tool. Also, with proper care and storage, this tool will last you for a lifetime.

Though many aviary builders use heavy staples of some kind for fastening the hardware cloth to a wood frame, these tend to pull loose in time, as the wood ages. Also, if you hit the staple one time too many times with the hammer, the staple will break the wire it is covering, destroying the staple's fastening strength. The heavy-duty staplers that are so easy to use can result in the same types of problems. Staples at least are a fairly easy type of fastener to remove, should you need to disassemble the aviary at a future time in order to move it to a new location.

Roofing nails are the most effective means I have found for attaching the quarter-inch mesh hardware cloth to a wood frame. Use the hot galvanized type of roofing nail for the longest life without danger of rusting or corrosion. Each nail covers four welds in the wire, and as the roofing nails are slightly serrated, they will not easily pull out of the wood. The only time these nails will pull loose is if the wood frame warps badly when aging, exerting a huge amount of pressure on the wire and the nail. Roofing nails of several lengths are available in any hardware store. As the shorter ones will pull out of the wood more easily with any pressure, use roofing nails that are at least one inch in length for best long-term results.

When placing a piece of the hardware cloth for nailing, first adjust the piece to the correct position and tack the top center of the piece in place. Then go to the bottom center of the piece, adjust it to the correct location, tighten the piece to its maximum and then tack the bottom center in place. After this, the right and left center should be stretched tight and tacked down. Working from these four secured points, you will be able to place the remainder of the nails along the four sides of the piece of hardware cloth without getting a crimp or overlap in the hardware cloth. Place double nails in the corners of each piece of hardware cloth for added security in heavy winds and stresses, and at intervals of about one foot along each edge of the hardware cloth.

For more permanent fastening, you can use screws with large heads, or widen the screw head's coverage with a washer. Screws require a pilot hole drilled in a size considerably smaller than the shaft of the screw in order to function to their full capabilities. Nevertheless, if the pilot hole is too small, the screw will split the wood as it goes in. Screws are available in a huge variety of sizes and lengths to suit any purpose you might have in building the aviary. Electric drills and screwdrivers are now available that make drilling these pilot holes and the attachment of the screws a very easy process. However, this is a rather expensive way of attaching hardware cloth to a wood frame, and unless you use stainless steel screws, you will still have the problem of eventual rusting. Roofing nails are far cheaper and are likely to last for the life of the aviary.

Attaching the quarter-inch mesh hardware cloth to a metal frame is more time-consuming, but also is a much more permanent method for the construction of the aviary. For this method of fastening, the best means of attaching the hardware cloth is through the use of nuts and bolts. The heads and nuts for the small bolts are wide enough to securely fasten the quarter-inch mesh hardware cloth, and as a result, you will probably not have to use a small washer, in addition, to be sure that the wire is securely fastened. Push the bolt through the wire and the hole in the metal frame, and put the nut on the end of the bolt. Tighten the nut, and the hardware cloth will be completely secure in anything except a tornado, major earthquake or a vehicle crashing into the aviary.

You can also use a piece of heavy wire to fasten the hardware cloth to the metal frame, of course, but this is not very attractive. In addition, if the pressure of the wire is too great, a wire can cut through the individual wires in the hardware cloth. A piece of wire of a heavy enough gauge to perform this function will probably be too stiff to bend with your fingers. You'll need a pair of pliers for grasping the wire and twisting it until it is tight. This is not a very effective method for fastening hardware cloth to the framing of your aviary.

HALF-INCH MESH HARDWARE CLOTH

The second type of wire that you can use on an aviary is the half-inch mesh hardware cloth. Because of the danger that snakes and mice will squeeze through hardware cloth of this size, I do not recommend it for outdoor use, except for very large birds, such as pheasants, ducks or chickens. Snakes and mice are two of the greatest dangers to your smaller birds, and you need to exclude them at any cost. Using the half-inch mesh hardware cloth for indoor use should be safe, though there is still the danger of mice gaining access to the aviary.

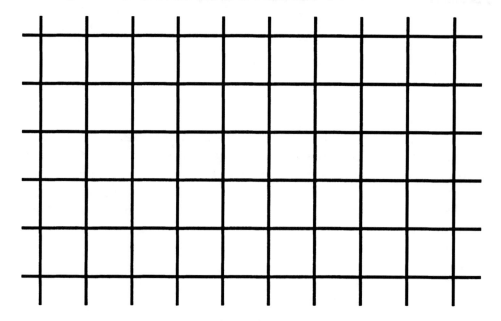

Illustration of 1/2 inch mesh hardware cloth

Half-inch mesh hardware cloth comes in the same widths that you will find in the quarter-inch mesh, usually from 18 inches to four feet. Again, the 36-inch and 48-inch widths are the commonest and the most economical to buy. The full rolls are one hundred feet in length, and most large hardware stores carry it as a standard item. Of course, you can always buy less than a full roll, and most hardware stores that carry the hardware cloth will be willing to cut pieces to size for you. As it is extremely bulky to display on the floor, you will probably have to ask for it. Most stores will stock hardware cloth in the back storage area where it is not in the way and can easily be rolled out and cut for any customer that needs it. Again, the smaller stores may carry rolls in lengths of 25 feet for smaller aviary projects. Nevertheless, the cheapest way to buy hardware cloth always is through buying a full roll. Also, if you are willing to wait on a special order and buy several rolls for cash, most stores will give you a worthwhile discount on the purchase.

Fastening the half-inch mesh to the aviary frame can be accomplished in the same manner that you would use to fasten the quarter-inch mesh hardware cloth. For wood frames, this means staples or roofing nails. For metal frames, the use of nuts, washers and bolts is the best. The half-inch mesh hardware cloth is also much cheaper than the quarter-inch mesh. Yet, the additional safety factor provided by the quarter-inch mesh is well worth the additional cost.

HALF-INCH BY ONE INCH MESH WELDED WIRE

A third commonly used aviary covering is the half-inch by one-inch mesh welded wire. This also comes in rolls of 100 feet, and because of the heavier gauge of the wire used in its manufacture, this type of wire is quite a bit more expensive than the hardware cloth. It is also easier to handle when fastening it to the framing, since the gauge of the wire is heavier. The manufacturing process results in a much more even and squared off piece of wire to use in your aviary construction than it is possible to get with the hardware cloth. The thinner wire of the hardware cloth is much more flexible and more difficult to handle during its manufacture, and the defects in many of the manufactured rolls prevent you from having a perfect edge or corner on the piece of hardware cloth that you're using.

The heavier gauge of wire used in the manufacture of this type of aviary covering is also more difficult to cut, and most tools that will cut the individual wires will also leave a sharp point that will be dangerous to you and to the birds. Cutting this wire with the use of a pair of the large tinsnips recommended for cutting the hardware cloth is possible, but as this will also leave sharp points and dangerous edges, you would need to follow this first cutting with a second trimming of the individual wires, using a small pair of wirecutters of the type used by electricians. You can get a pair of these wirecutters that has one perfectly smooth edge. When you use this to cut the sharp points off of the wire at an angle, it will leave the edges of the welded wire as safe as it is possible to make it, and also much easier to work with. For additional safety and neatness, you can use a fine file to round and smooth the final edge where you have cut the welded wire.

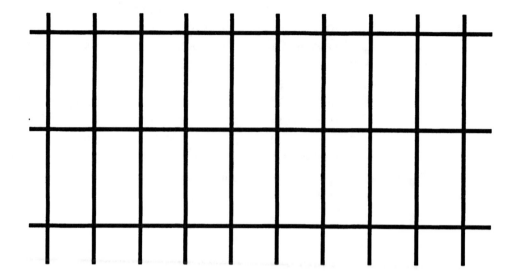

Illustration of 1/2 inch by one inch welded wire

The primary disadvantages of using wire of this size is first of all the danger of snakes and mice getting into the aviary through the wire. A snake small enough to squeeze through this wire is also large enough to catch and eat birds the size of grass parakeets and Java Rice Birds. Mice can readily pass through this wire mesh, and though they are usually of no danger to the adult birds, they will eat eggs and babies, as well as eating and fouling the birds' feed. The bacteria that live in the mammalian digestive tract are different from the ones found in the avian digestive tract. When the birds pick up these new and dangerous microorganisms from the mice, they will soon become ill. Without a fast treatment with a powerful germ-killer such as chlorine to rid their digestive systems of these dangerous bacteria, the birds will die.

The second major disadvantage of this ½ by 1 inch welded wire is that most types are not galvanized, but only treated to prevent immediate rusting. As a result, this wire will rust rapidly if placed outdoors and exposed to sun, rain and the oxygen in the air. If you plan to use this welded wire outdoors for larger birds that will be able to kill any snakes or mice in their areas, you will have to treat it in some way to prevent rusting. This can create more health problems if you are keeping birds that will chew on the wire of the aviary. These birds are also likely to chew on the paint or preservative you've applied to the wire, and may poison themselves in this way. The larger jays, toucans, and the larger gallinaceous birds will be able to kill any snake or mouse that can squeeze through this wire to get into your aviary. All you will then have to worry about is that the snake will eat the birds' eggs before the birds can kill the snake! See Chapter 5 on Varmint Proofing and Aviary Security for a thorough discussion of predators and how to protect the aviary from them.

ONE-HALF BY THREE INCH WELDED WIRE

This same type of welded wire also comes in a ½ X 3 inch mesh. This type of welded wire is even more stiff than the ½ in by 1 inch size, as the wire is made from individual wires of a coarser gauge. Again, I don't recommend the use of outdoor aviary wire of this size for the same reasons that were covered in the previous paragraphs. Any comments that applied to the ½ X 1 inch mesh wire will also apply to this ½ X 3 inch mesh wire.

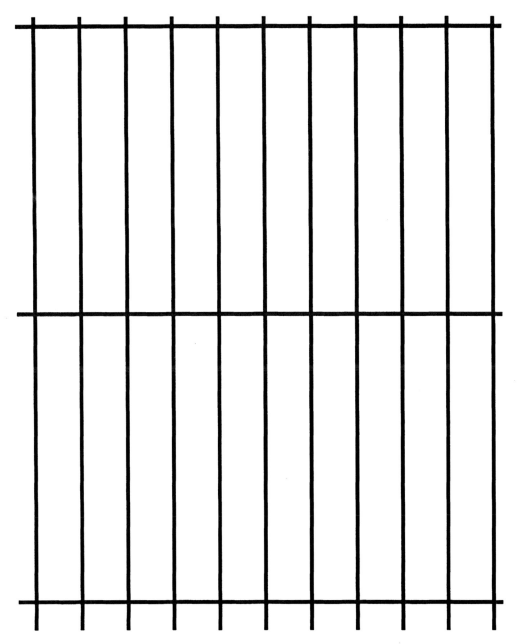

Illustration of 1/2 inch by 3 inch welded wire

ONE-INCH BY ONE-INCH WELDED WIRE

This type of welded aviary wire also is available in a 1 inch by 1 inch size, as illustrated below. The wire gauge is the same size that is used in the ½ X 1 welded wire, and the strengths and disadvantages are also the same. However, the very fact that the opening is wider will allow even larger predators to enter the aviary through this 1 X 1 inch wire mesh. Use this size of wire on an outdoor aviary only when you can be absolutely certain that the birds within will still be safe and secure, along with their eggs and their nestlings. Murphy's Law will assure that if you are raising silky chickens and Rothschild's Mynahs in the same aviary, a predator gaining entrance will completely ignore the chickens and will be sure to attack and kill the mynahs. On two occasions, I have had a similar situation occur, and twice burned is triply aware of the possibility of predators gaining access to the birds.

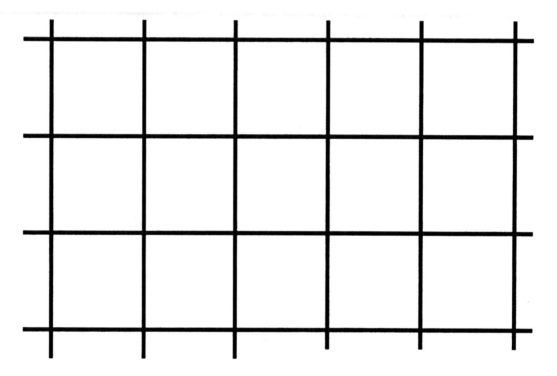

Illustration of one inch by one inch welded wire

Aviary wire of a larger mesh, such as the galvanized fencing often used for cockatoos and macaws, is suitable only for birds of this size and with the full ability to protect themselves. Still, a nocturnal rat will easily get through this large mesh wire, and is fully capable of killing an adult macaw and will certainly consider macaw eggs and babies a great delicacy. Please read Chapter 5 carefully, and use the benefit of my own experience to protect all of your birds that are maintained in an outdoor aviary.

There is no area in the temperate or tropical zones of the world that is safe from predators of some sort. They are a part of the balance of nature, and you may have to go to extremes to protect your birds from their presence and predation.

One of the most recently developed meshes for aviary netting is a very fine stainless steel mesh, actually woven into a form that looks at first glance like hardware cloth. However this mesh is not welded, but woven of fine, stainless steel wire, and it is extremely flexible. This product goes by the brand name of Zoomesh®, and it is made in two strengths. You can get more information on this product from the manufacturer, Kettner & Associates (800) 334-5330. Though this mesh will not be satisfactory for the large parrot-type birds, it will be an excellent aviary netting when you can assure that no large predators will be clawing at it or climbing on it. Its major asset is its flexibility, and a panicked bird flying into it at full speed is unlikely to damage its body seriously. Also, the mesh of this material is small enough that no potentially dangerous predator will ever be able to get through it. The mesh on this netting appears to be approximately 1/8 of an inch in diameter. As it is made of stainless steel, only tearing, clawing or the pressure of a falling tree will be likely to damage it, and it will not rust or disintegrate under any normal weather conditions.

Another type of galvanized wire mesh is also available in ½ inch, 1 inch and 2 inch meshes. This is used extensively for domestic poultry and is usually just called "chicken wire". Most hardware stores and farm and feed stores will carry this product. The main advantage to this type of wire mesh is its very reasonable price, because of its universal usage for chicken coops and poultry pens. As it is galvanized, it will also last for many years without rusting. The pattern for the ½ inch mesh is illustrated on the next page, and other sizes are similar in appearance, with larger openings to form the mesh of the wire.

Only the smallest size, the one-half inch mesh, would be suitable for small birds, and it is called aviary mesh. Unfortunately, small mice will be able to squeeze through even this half-inch mesh easily, and they will grow very rapidly in the bounty that they find in a well kept aviary. A snake large enough to eat any of the small birds, and the eggs and young of larger birds will also be able to get through this half-inch mesh wire with no problem at all. Never forget that a snake in the aviary is a disaster in the making.

The one-inch mesh is in common use for commercial poultry and game birds, and it is one of least expensive forms of aviary wire available. However, many of the finches, warblers, tits, hummingbirds and other small birds will be able to go right through this one-inch mesh. Even chipmunks can squeeze through this mesh easily, and though they will not bother the birds, they will eat and carry away all of the bird feed in the aviary. This is not a suitable aviary wire unless you are raising larger softbills that will view snakes, mice, and even chipmunks as delectable treats. The one-inch mesh is not suitable for any of the smaller birds.

The two-inch mesh is often used for chickens and other domestic fowl, but it is not useful for most aviary applications. Though the large birds may be safe enough in an enclosure of two-inch mesh wire, anything smaller than a toucan will be in deadly danger in an enclosure using two-inch mesh wire. Even rats can squeeze through this wire with no trouble, and even if they are not a danger to the large birds physically, their nocturnal searching for food will panic the birds at night. Also, the larger psittacines will bite holes in this wire very easily. The only advantage of this type of two-inch mesh wire is that it is very flexible if a bird should fly into it, and the bird will not be injured. All things considered, I do not recommend this size of wire for any type of aviary construction for exotic birds.

If you are using an alcove as an aviary entrance, depending on the size of the birds you keep, you can use larger mesh wire on the alcove. The larger mesh will be cheaper and will still hold any birds temporarily. For finches, you can put half-inch mesh wire on the alcove, but do not use the one-inch mesh, as most finches can go right through it.

The following illustrates the pattern found in the chicken wire discussed above

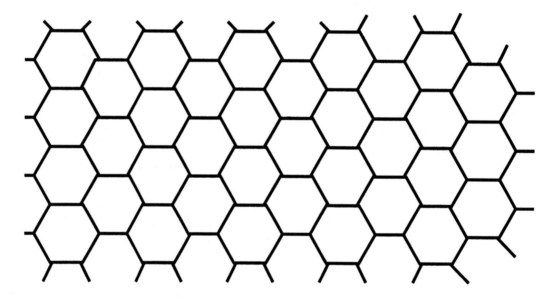

Chapter 5

Varmint-Proofing and Aviary Security

The greatest danger to any of the birds maintained in an outdoor aviary will undoubtedly come from animals that normally and instinctively prey on birds. To these creatures, the birds in a small area that they can't escape seem to be the easiest of prey. Any dangers resulting from adverse weather conditions, active criminal theft, or accidental aviary destruction are far less likely to occur. If you don't consciously decide and act to exclude these creatures from the aviary in your initial planning, your birds will be easy prey for these predators, and you will have continual problems with frequent serious injuries, dead birds, and abandoned nests. Birds that do not feel safe and secure in their aviaries will never make any attempt to breed.

Domestic animals and pets can be a continual problem around an outdoor aviary either in a town or in a rural area unless you take positive steps to exclude them. Domestic cats are by far the worst problem that most breeders encounter when keeping birds in an aviary. Even people who keep their dogs well trained and under control in their own areas often allow cats to run free and harass every bird in the neighborhood. Feral cats that belong to no one and must hunt and kill for their own continued existence can be a continual problem even in the rural areas that are far removed from the concentrated populations of towns and cities. Cats climb very well, and they are active nocturnally, a combination that means disaster for the birds in your aviaries that are not protected.

Wild creatures are present in far more variety and can include everything from mice and rats to a bewildering variety of raptors, snakes and mammals. Every area has its own varieties of reptiles and mammals that look upon the birds in your aviaries as fair game. Raptors in the form of hawks in the daytime and owls at night represent a source of continuing panic to your birds in an enclosed aviary. Only in Alaska and Hawaii will you be free from the danger of snakes. This chapter will discuss the various ways you can use to exclude these potential predators from your aviaries.

Always keep in mind that the predators that will continually harass the birds in your aviaries are only doing what nature intended. Birds are their natural prey, and an enclosed aviary from which the birds cannot escape is an open invitation to a whole variety of natural predators. Blaming these predators for their natural instincts is nothing if not shortsighted. Nature intended for them to prey at least partly on birds, and they will continue to do this despite any of our own adverse opinions or angry denunciations. Rather, we need to strive continually to keep the aviary as a safe haven for the birds we maintain by doing everything in our power to keep them protected from all of the local predators, both wild and domestic.

As I mentioned in Chapter 4, from long and sad experience in a variety of areas of the United States, the only aviary wire or netting that I have found to be safe for even the tiniest birds is the quarter-inch mesh hardware cloth. Nothing that can be of any serious danger to the birds is able to get through this quarter-inch mesh wire. If you have installed the wire tightly over the framework to eliminate any spaces that a mouse or snake might squeeze through, your birds should have no predators to deal with that have come through the wire and into the aviary.

Any larger mesh wire will admit small snakes that are perfectly capable of eating eggs and nestlings, even if they are too small to eat a fully adult bird. The half-inch mesh hardware cloth is suitable only for large birds that will attack and eat a snake or mouse on sight. Mice easily squeeze through the half-inch mesh hardware cloth, and a snake large enough to eat a bird as large as a cardinal or grosbeak can also easily squeeze through the half-inch mesh. If you are raising toucans, mice and small snakes are mere delicacies for their diet. However, if you are raising the waxbills, grassfinches or mannikins, snakes and mice in the aviary are an absolute disaster.

Using the quarter-inch mesh hardware cloth, however, is only the first step in protecting the birds in your aviary. If you have left a quarter inch gap around the door into the aviary, mice and fairly large snakes will gain easy access to the aviary around the door. When you build the door to the aviary, make sure that the door closes tightly. There is a happy medium between a door that is so tight that it swells and jams in the frame during wet weather, and a door so loose that a five-foot snake can squeeze under it. A one-eighth inch gap between the door and the framing is ideal, as nothing large enough to harm the birds seriously will squeeze through this space, and a wooden door will not swell so much in wet weather that it jams or freezes in the frame. The worst pests in my own aviaries were the snakes that were able to flatten themselves sufficiently to squeeze under the aviary doors.

As wood ages in both the door and the framing, it can crack, chip or warp and leave a gap large enough to admit a variety of small predators. Check your doors frequently for signs of warping or of gaps developing. Even a knot falling out of a piece of lumber might leave a hole big enough for a mouse or rat to enter the aviary. Minor problems of this type can be corrected by using a small shim to fill the space or by filling a gap or hole in the wood with exterior spackling compound.

In addition, it is always a good idea to put hardware cloth over your aviary framing before putting on any roofing material. In a severe storm, any type of roofing that has been used on an aviary can blow off. If the hardware cloth is still secure beneath the roofing, your birds will not be able to escape. Without this additional hardware cloth coverage, a storm that blows a piece of roofing material off of your aviary will allow all of the birds in the aviary to escape.

Though you can protect your aviaries and the birds within them from any normal storm, our country is plagued by two types of far stronger natural windstorms that will mean the probable destruction of your aviary, as well as your home. These are hurricanes and tornadoes. Should you live in an area in the east and your area receives warning of a bad hurricane approaching, the best thing you can do is to catch up all of your aviary birds, place them in small cages temporarily, and place the cages in a hole or root cellar below ground level. Regardless of the ferocity of the wind, anything below ground level will be safe. For tornadoes which can occur through large areas of the United States, there is little or no warning and no protection except a root cellar or bomb shelter, and you are almost certain to lose the aviary and all of the birds in the aviary if a tornado passes directly through it.

This is an appropriate place to point out that the special strains of birds you have developed in your aviaries may be irreplaceable. Once you have developed the best and most successful breeding strain of a species, place a selection of the birds of this strain at a location several miles away with a friend or fellow breeder. Though your aviaries in all probability will be safe over the long term, having a selection of your best birds at an alternate location is a very valuable type of insurance to have in the event of a major disaster in your own aviaries.

Once you have the sides, roofing and doors of the aviary as secure as they can be, the next place requiring attention is the base of the aviary. Dirt is not a secure base for an aviary, and any number of small mammals dig and tunnel well enough to enter the aviary through the ground and under the walls. I once visited an aviary that had no ground protection. Though the owner had a wide variety of healthy finches, none of them were making any breeding efforts of any kind. The reason was obvious -- mouse holes were everywhere you looked, and mice were peeking out of several of them on a sunny day. At night, when the nocturnal mice came out in force to feed and scramble around the aviary, that aviary must have been a close approximation for an avian Hell all through the night.

The best way I have ever found to eliminate mice and other small or large burrowing creatures from the aviary is illustrated on the page 55. The only required material is a strip of 1/4 inch mesh hardware cloth approximately 18 inches wide. Also, for this purpose, you can use the cheaper 1/2 inch mesh hardware cloth, but be sure to use nothing with a mesh that is larger than 1/2 inch. Fasten this material to the outside base of the aviary, and then bury the hardware cloth around the aviary at an angle of 45° or more, all the way around the aviary, including the area where the door is located. Once this hardware cloth is buried and the ditch is filled in, it will be completely invisible. However, any mouse, rat, mole, ground squirrel, prairie dog chipmunk, or any other burrowing animal that tries to dig into the aviary will run into this barrier of buried hardware cloth. Fortunately, no small animal has the reasoning ability to back up, dig deeper, and go under the hardware cloth, and this hardware cloth will totally frustrate their efforts to enter the aviary. I maintained a set of 16 large aviaries, each one protected in this manner, and in nine years never had any kind of small animal gain access to any of those aviaries.

Though it might be possible to exclude these burrowing creatures by using a thick concrete base for the aviary, this would be a far more expensive way of solving the problem. Also, mice and rats can in time chew through a concrete barrier, but they can never chew or tunnel through the hardware cloth. I used a concrete floor on one aviary once, and found it so unsatisfactory for a variety of reasons that this is the only time I have ever used a concrete base for an aviary. All other aviaries have had bases of natural soil protected by the hardware cloth.

The buried hardware cloth will also exclude larger animals, such as dogs or foxes, that attempt to dig into the aviary. However, the larger animals are far more likely to panic the birds in the aviary. Since these animals are not climbers, a fence around the aviary is the most likely method of providing protection for the birds. A fence just four feet tall will prevent these animals from getting close enough to the aviary to panic the birds.

Climbing animals, such as cats, opossums and raccoons, are much more difficult to exclude, as they are all nocturnal and will climb a fence and will also climb up the wall of the aviary. Any animal this large climbing on the aviary at night will panic the birds within the aviary. While nest sleepers away from the aviary wire will probably continue to sit tight, any perching birds that are anywhere close to the wire side of the aviary are sure to panic. If one bird in an aviary panics at night and flies into the aviary wire, it will in turn panic every other bird in the aviary.

Nothing is more destructive to your breeding efforts than night panics in the aviary. Panicking birds will destroy the nests of other birds as they fly wildly into them in the dark, and any bird that is frightened off of the nest at night will abandon that nest. This means eggs lost and even babies abandoned and lost.

Since the unknown is the greatest source of panic, birds in a completely dark aviary for the night are the most likely to panic and kill themselves as they fly headlong into the wire or framing of the aviary. The best suggestion I have seen to counteract this is through placing a small, 25 watt red or blue incandescent light bulb in one corner of the aviary. Even a standard white bulb is satisfactory. A bulb of this size will produce no more light than a full moon, but still allows the birds to see what is going on around them when they are awakened by a noise during the night. A bird that can see a danger and knows that the danger cannot reach it is far less likely to panic than a bird that hears a noise in pitch darkness and takes off in instinctive, panicked flight in order to get away from the terrifying, unknown noise of a potential predator.

The only possible way to exclude these climbing predators is probably to attach an electrical wire around the aviary at about the two-foot level. Any animal that attempts to climb up the side of the aviary will receive a rude shock when it comes into contact with the electrical wire. And again, no animal would have enough reasoning ability to jump a full two feet over the wire to begin its climb up the aviary wall. Birds are unlikely to panic at the sounds of a night prowler below them; only when the sounds come to be even with them or above them in the aviary are they certain to panic. The electric fencing materials that are sold at any large feed store are adaptable for this method of aviary protection, and this is certainly the best method for excluding the climbing animals from the aviary.

Illustration of below ground aviary varmint protection

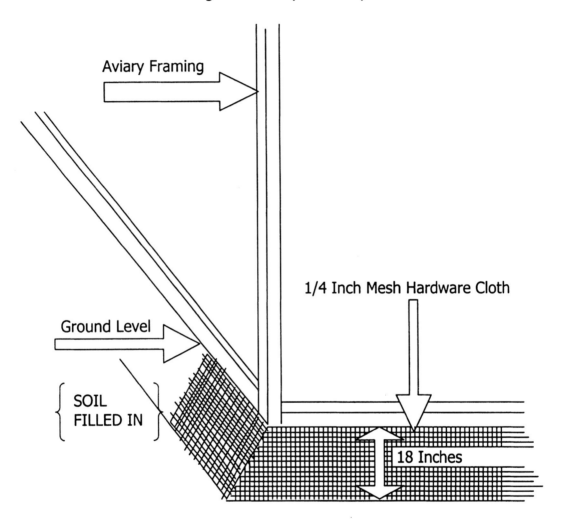

For the security of the birds, it is crucially important to place the nesting receptacles in the aviary away from the outside walls of the aviary. The methods for doing this will be covered in detail in Chapter 10. Likewise, all perches and plantings should be placed away from the sides of the aviary, as I have covered in detail in Chapter 9 and Chapter 11.

Another possible way to minimize the danger to the aviary birds from climbing predators on the outside of the aviary is to place solid, fairly slippery material around the outside of the upper half of the aviary. A variety of clear or opaque roofing materials are available on the market that you can use for this purpose, as Chapter 1 covered in detail. Any of the fiberglass or polycarbonate sheeting would be good for this purpose.

Flying predators will present you with a completely different problem. During the daylight hours, hawks are likely to target your aviary and the birds within it. They will dive and hit the hardware cloth of the aviary and will in the process panic every bird within the aviary. Raptors are not intelligent birds, and they never seem to realize that they cannot gain access to these delicious birds through the aviary wire. A raptor is unlikely to give up and quit when its natural avian prey is so close. A hawk will literally starve itself to death by attacking only the aviary and attempting to find prey nowhere else. Nature has developed these birds as efficient killing machines, but they are notably lacking in brain power. In time, the birds in the aviary will become used to the attacks of these predators, and will barely flinch when the hawk hits the aviary.

An owl that hits the aviary after dark is the one creature against which there is no logical and truly effective protection. Clear fiberglass or polycarbonate sheeting on the roof and upper half of the aviary will be the only protective measure that will possibly be effective against the attacks of an owl.

Though through the years, my aviaries have suffered attacks by a bewildering variety of wild and domesticated creatures. About the only wild creatures that have not yet put in an appearance are bobcat, cougar and bear. As powerful and strong as these predators are, there is no aviary protection that is likely to be effective against them, should they target the birds or food items in your aviary.

As a final note, even the smallest creatures that enter your aviaries may cause problems with your birds and your breeding efforts, but a problem can also turn out to be a blessing in disguise. At one time, I was raising quaker parakeets, *Myiopsitta monachus*. The pairs were using a cockatiel type nestbox, and I was able to check the nests easily to see how the quakers' breeding efforts were progressing. When the babies hatched and were a few days old, I noted a lesion or sore on the abdomen of a couple of the babies. This was quite puzzling until I dug into the nesting material and found some little black beetles and worms that were the obvious cause of the damage. When I sent a sample of these beetles and worms to the State Entomology Laboratory, the identification came back as the Lesser Mealworm, *Alphitobius diaperinus*. Well, mealworms or not, they were unwelcome in the Quakers' nestboxes. Once I gathered some of the beetles and worms for culturing, I treated the nestboxes with Malathion®, a potent insecticide that I knew to be deadly to the insects, but harmless for the birds.

The Lesser Mealworms were more easily cultured that the standard mealworm, *Tenebrio molitor*. With a cover for the container to keep the Lesser Mealworm beetles from flying away, these little insects were happy to breed and supply me with all of the Lesser Mealworms that I needed for all of the finches in the aviaries.

Chapter 6

Entrances
Single Doors, Double Doors and Alcoves

Any aviary has to have a way for you to enter it in order to feed the birds and for any cleaning, maintenance, nest checks or changes that are necessary. As you will almost certainly be entering the aviary on a daily basis and probably several times a day, the method you choose in constructing this entrance is certain to be of lasting importance. Reading this chapter before you begin your construction may save you a lot of problems that might otherwise only become apparent at a later date.

As is true with all of the types of aviary construction, each method of entrance construction will have its own advantages and disadvantages. Knowing what these advantages and disadvantages are before you begin construction is important, as this knowledge will keep you from doing extensive reconstruction at a later date should you decide that the method of entrance construction you have used is not the best one possible for your own location and your own purposes.

Providing double doors with an alcove between has been the accepted standard for building an entrance to an aviary for many years. Most outdoor aviaries have an entrance alcove of some type, with two doors – one door for entering the alcove that can be closed before the second door is opened to permit access to the aviary. This, in theory, prevents the loss of birds that manage to fly past you when you are entering or leaving the aviary. In my experience, there are two primary advantages of this system of using double doors with an alcove in between the doors.

The first and most important advantage I have found is that this alcove is an ideal place into which you can herd a group of birds, then close the door behind you. This allows you to catch the birds far more easily than you could ever manage to catch them in the large aviary itself. Once the birds are in this small area, you can easily catch the ones you want to remove, then release the remaining birds back into the main aviary. This alcove catching area limits panicking to that small area and makes catching the birds far faster and easier. Catching the birds in this alcove also relieves you of the necessity of chasing birds all around the main aviary, which is all too likely to damage plants, perches and nesting sites and to disrupt the breeding efforts of the birds that you want to leave in the aviary. If you have built the top of the alcove at the same level as the top of the aviary, this corralling and catching method will work very well. If the top of the alcove is lower than the top of the aviary, you will have a great deal of trouble herding the birds into the alcove for catching.

Another important use I have found for these alcoves is for food storage. Non-perishable foods such as seeds and grit can be stored in sealed containers in these alcoves, even in totally unprotected areas outdoors. The galvanized metal garbage cans are an ideal, waterproof container that I have often used for this purpose. Plastic containers can also serve this purpose, of course, but plastics that are exposed to the sun and weather for long periods become very brittle and they will crack and break easily. They are not satisfactory for long-term outdoor storage. Also, mice and rats cannot get to the food when it is kept in galvanized metal containers, but they will chew holes in plastic or wood containers to get at the free food within them.

These containers in the alcove make the food very handy and accessible when you are refilling the feeders in the aviary. You can also use these containers to store extra nesting receptacles, short perches, extra feeding containers, or any other item that you might be using in the aviary. I've often kept containers of dried eggshells in these containers which are broken up and scattered for the birds to allow them a ready source of available calcium in their diet.

When you have a bank of several aviaries joined side by side to save on framing and wire, you can construct a single, long alcove to serve all of the aviary doors. This method of construction would be far cheaper and more effective than constructing a double door and alcove for each of a number of separate outdoor aviaries. This will still provide you with a secure storage area, and a location for catching the birds when that becomes necessary. This will be a long and narrow catching area, of course, and you will have a great deal more difficulty catching birds in this type of alcove than you will have in a small alcove entrance to only one aviary, unless you have placed a door periodically that can close the long alcove into smaller sections.

One disadvantage of the double door and alcove entrance is the fact that the materials will add significantly to the overall cost of construction for the outdoor aviary. The additional wire or hardware cloth and framing that you will use for the construction of this alcove could also be used for the construction of another small aviary or large cage for birds that cannot be kept with the ones for which you have designed the main aviary.

As far as preventing the loss of birds, I have found these alcoves to be totally unsatisfactory. Forgetting to latch the outside door even once is an invitation for it to blow open in the breeze while you are feeding with the second door open. The birds will take advantage of this instantly and will proceed to fly out through the alcove to freedom. It is possible prevent this by installing a spring on each of the alcove doors to be certain that they will close behind you when you enter or leave the aviary. This will add to the cost of constructing the aviary alcove, of course.

Believe me, over a number of years, no matter how careful you are, you will at some point lose birds through the double doors of an alcove. I have lost dozens of birds in this manner over the years, enough that I will never again use a double alcove for an aviary entrance. The extra expense and time required for building the double doors and alcove are simply not worth the effort, when you are likely to lose birds through them anyway.

As an alternative, I have defied the conventional wisdom for aviary building and now use a single door exclusively on all of my aviaries. The single door that I recommend should be about two feet shorter than the height of the aviary. That means that if the aviary is seven feet tall, your entrance door should be only five feet tall. This, of course, means that most people will have to bend over to enter the aviary. Those with bald or shaved heads should wear a hat when entering and leaving the aviary through this single, low door, or a skinned head at least once a month is almost a certainty. When the birds fly toward this door, they will fly at the highest point in the aviary and will therefore fly above the door and not through it. If you also place a perch in this space above the door, the birds will always head for that high perch, and you will never lose one that flies low enough to fly through the aviary door.

In all the years that I have used this type of a single door, I have only had two birds fly out past me when entering or leaving the aviary. Both were very young birds that could not fly well and could not gain altitude easily, and I was able to recapture both with a net outside the aviary. Any birds with good flying ability will fly over you and over the door to the wire area above the single door, and this will keep them from escaping. This lower door is now what I use on all aviaries, for all types of birds. The low, single door is safe, effective, and the only possible loss or damage is to the top of the head when you neglect to bend over far enough on entering the aviary.

As you build the aviary, you will need to decide the location for the door and then install the necessary solid framing to support the door. Once this framing is secure, you can measure the interior dimensions of the framing and build your door to fit those dimensions. As you measure, be certain to allow for a full one-half inch of clearance before you begin to cut the dimensions for the door itself. This one-half inch clearance recommendation applies to both the horizontal measurement and the vertical measurement for the door. Any less space for clearance than this is likely to cause the door to stick somewhere along its edge at a later date. This clearance, after all, will leave only a one-quarter inch of clearance on each side of the door.

This allowance for clearance is absolutely necessity to have the doors on your aviary open and close easily with a small space on the top, bottom and sides, as I also discussed in Chapter 1 concerning the outdoor aviary. Though a door that sticks to the framing on one edge will be no problem in warmer climates, when you have a tight door in areas of freezing weather, this is sure to create a difficult problem for you. Freezing nights often follow a rainy winter weather front in many of the areas in North America. This rain will cause the wood to become very wet, and the wood is sure to expand as it soaks up water. This dampness and expansion will turn a door that is already sticky into a very tight door. When the temperature goes below freezing, the door will freeze shut to the point that you will not be able to open it without tearing out the side of the aviary.

Should you have a door freeze shut unexpectedly, before you cut a hole in the wire to get into the aviary, you may be able to use an alternate method to get the door open. Fill a standard metal watering can with hot water, and gradually pour it around the door and its framing. This hot water will gradually thaw the frozen wood, but you may have to use more than one can of hot water. Within a few minutes, the door will be thawed enough that you will be able to pull it open. In order to prevent this from happening again, immediately use a tool to plane the door down to the point where it will swing freely, even when soaking wet. If you cannot maneuver a wood plane around the door to do this, you can use either a drawknife or a hammer and wood chisel to do the job.

When you design any door for an aviary, you will need to buy the necessary hardware to install the door and then more hardware in order to use the door, once it is installed. Before you begin this installation, however, be sure to test the completed door in the open space that you have prepared for it first. The door should fit, even allowing for the width of the hinges once installed, with at least one-eighth of an inch clearance on the top, bottom, and side opposite the hinges. This will allow for the certain expansion of the wood door when it gets wet, so that you will still be able to open the door.

With metal doors, of course, the expansion that occurs will be far less. In addition, the expansion will not occur in wet weather nor in cold weather, but rather during the hottest days of the summer. Metal doors will also collect the heat, and a metal door that has been in the direct sunlight for several hours on a hot day actually may become too hot to touch.

Hinges of some type are the first necessary pieces of hardware that you will have to install once the door is measured, built and tested. Hinges are available in all sizes and styles to fit the design of your aviary and most hinges come with a set of screws for installing them. When you have chosen the type of hinges you want and are ready to install them, you will need to install these hinges securely on the door before lifting the door into position in its prepared framing.

When you settle on the location for the hinges on the door, check the frame to be absolutely sure that there is no knot or other flaw in the wood on the frame that will cause a problem in installing the door into the frame. If you note a knot at the location where the hinge will be installed, move the hinge on the door to a position so that the screws for the hinge are sure to miss this knot. If for some reason, you must put the fastening screw into a knot, you will have to drill a pilot hole nearly the diameter of the screw to accommodate that screw. Otherwise, you will not be able to install the screw into this extremely hard area of the wood.

Should you build a metal aviary, you can use special bolts to fasten your hinges, hooks and hasps. Any large hardware store carries the type of machine screws with a beveled head that will do the same job in your metal framed aviary as the beveled wood screws do for the wood framed aviary. For most applications, the short, quarter inch machine screws are quite adequate for fastening the hardware on the doors of your metal framed aviary. The same fastening recommendation holds true for any type of hasp or fastener that you install to keep the door of the aviary securely closed.

If you live in a cold, snowy climate area, snow may collect in front of the door deeply enough to block the door. When this happens, do not use the door itself to knock the snow aside far enough to open the door. Using the door as a snow shovel in this manner will put a tremendous strain on the door's hinges. In very little time in a wood framed aviary, you will find that the screws that fasten the hinges are pulling out of the wood from the pressure you are exerting on the snow. This means reattaching the door later and more securely. It is far better and easier to keep a shovel handy to remove the snow from in front of the door. By using a shovel, you can clear away the snow, allow the door to open freely, and save yourself the trouble of replacing the screws that hold the door in place and allow it to swing open and closed freely.

Be sure to use hinges that are large enough to support the size and weight of your aviary door. Once you have the door with its installed hinges placed correctly in the frame, it is usually best to use a small nail tapped in with a hammer and then pulled out to form a pilot hole for the screw. You can also use a small push drill or electric drill to drill a small pilot hole for the screw. This will enable you to start the screw far more easily, and the first screw in the framing is always the hardest and most awkward to get started. Once one screw is installed to hold the door at the proper level and position, the rest will go in much more easily. After installing the door, be sure to swing it back and forth to test the closing and clearance. If the wooden door is catching on any surface, this is the time to plane the door down to prevent the possibility of expansion in dampness and freezing that is discussed above.

When the door is installed and swinging freely, you are ready to install the rest of the hardware. The first necessity is a latch for both the outside and inside of the door. If the door will not be locked, you can use the simple hook and eye latches or one of the other types that are available in any hardware store. Should you plan on locking the aviary, you will need some type of a hasp that will accommodate the lock on the outside of the door. For the inside, the simpler latches will still be sufficient. You can also install a spring at this point to close the door behind you when you enter or leave the aviary. Still, it is vitally important to have some method of latching the door on both the inside and outside.

Locks are of value only in areas where children are present or will be playing. The lock will keep a fascinated child who really means no harm from opening the aviary and releasing the birds, where a simple latch that the child can reach will not prevent this type of mishap. If you have a number of aviaries, you can special order a group of small locks that will all take the same key. Most hardware stores have a special order department that will be happy to order as many as you think you will need. Specify the quantity that you want and also specify that the locks are to be 'keyed alike'. I have only had to use this method of locking aviaries in one location in which I lived, and that was to prevent interested visiting children from inadvertently opening the doors to the aviaries. Locks certainly do have their purpose in some aviary locations, but keep in mind that a lock will not stop a determined thief.

With your aviary door installed in the frame and prepared for latching both inside and outside the aviary, you are ready to put some type of handle on the door for easy opening and closing. Here again, there are a number of types of handles that you can install available in any hardware store. Check out what is available, and then install one handle for the outside of the door and then also one handle for the inside of the door. Before installing these handles, stand in front of the aviary and reach for the imaginary door handle. The point where you touch the aviary door is the point where you should install the handle. That will be the level at which you will feel most comfortable when you grab the handle to open the door after unlatching it.

Should you still decide to install an alcove for access to your aviary, there is one trick you can use to be certain that the birds will not voluntarily fly toward the alcove as you are entering or exiting the aviary. Install the alcove in a covered area of the aviary, and enclose it completely so that the alcove is much darker that the rest of the aviary. Zoological gardens frequently use this trick to allow their patrons to view the birds without any wire, glass or plastic in front of them to obstruct the view. The viewing area where the people are is simply a dark area, and the birds will never by choice fly into an area that is dark. Instinctively, all diurnal birds realize that darkness means danger. Only the few nocturnal species look upon darkness as their friend and their means of living safely.

Chapter 7

Building on a Slope

Most of our aviary locations are on reasonably flat land. A small amount of leveling is all that usually is necessary to prepare an area for the construction of an outdoor aviary. A level location of this type makes aviary building much easier and faster, as well as cheaper and less frustrating for a variety of reasons. When your home and aviary location is on a slope, you have no choice but to build on this slope, and this will require more work, knowledge, and expense than is required for flatland aviary construction.

As a first decision, you will need to look at the proposed location for the aviary on your area of sloping land. Then, you will have to decide whether it will be most advantageous to level the area first by terracing before you begin your construction to create a flat spot, or alternately to build the aviary into the slope, blending it with the landscape. There are advantages and disadvantages to each construction method, of course, and the purpose of this chapter is to discuss these methods in detail for your consideration should you ever find yourself with the need to build an aviary on land that is sloping twenty or thirty degrees, or with perhaps an even greater slope.

Should you decide to level the area by terracing, you will in effect be creating a flat location that will enable you to proceed to build a standard aviary as you would on flat land. However, in the location where you have dug out this terrace, before you begin construction, you will need to consider a few other factors that will be important in the construction and maintenance of a useful aviary that will be successful and operational for many years.

First, you need to widen out the level area of the terrace at your chosen location enough so that you can access all sides of the aviary easily. This wider area is necessary for both the initial construction and for any future maintenance that needs to be done on the outside of the aviary. As you will also surely need to maintain the terracing on all sides of the aviary, working from a flat spot by the aviary will also make this maintenance much easier. As you probably will make the aviary tall enough that you will need a ladder to access the top for installing both wire and solid covering, the terrace will need to be wide enough on all sides to accommodate a ladder so that it will be secure and stable either when standing free or leaning up against the aviary.

In addition, you will need to stabilize both the upper and lower levels of the terrace and the side areas around the aviary to prevent collapsing and erosion of the terracing caused by the varying weather conditions. The most critical area is the upper level of the terrace. You will need to stabilize this area with a wall of rock, brick, treated lumber, or block to keep the soil from collapsing and washing down onto the upper side of the aviary. The steeper your slope, the higher will be the upper terrace wall with which you will have to contend. Also, a steeper slope means a great deal of additional weight in soil and rocks that can come sliding down onto the upper side of your aviary after a heavy rain or deep snowfall. This weight can and will collapse the upper side of the aviary if you give it any chance at all to do this.

A heavy, reinforced wall will protect the upper side of the aviary and will keep the dirt and rocks on the upper slope from cascading down onto the side of your aviary. On a heavily forested slope, there is little likelihood of a serious mudslide down onto your aviary. However, grassy slopes are far less stable, and you may need to make additional terracing efforts to prevent the soil from coming loose in heavy rains to flow down onto your aviary. Many people who have built their homes at the base of a steep, grassy slope have lived to regret their choice of location after a period of heavy rains. A home destroyed by a mudslide or filled with mud even if it is not totally destroyed is no fun at all. Yet, people continue to insist on building their homes at the base of an insecure slope, which is definitely a bad decision and places the home directly in harm's way.

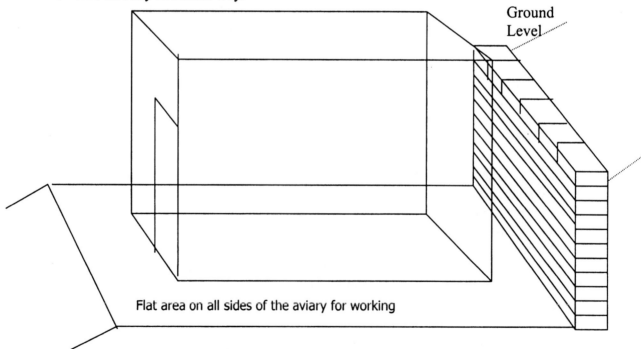

Ground Level

Flat area on all sides of the aviary for working

Drawing of an aviary with a single terrace

As an alternate way of handling the slope above your aviary, instead of a single reinforcing wall, you can use a stairstep type of terracing. Even if the slope is as great as 45°, you can develop each stairstep terrace to go up one foot high. If your one foot high retaining wall is six inches thick, this will still leave a six inch planting space for you to work with, before you then start the next one foot high terrace. This works quite well and still relieves most of the soil pressure that would be far greater on a single wall terrace for the slope.

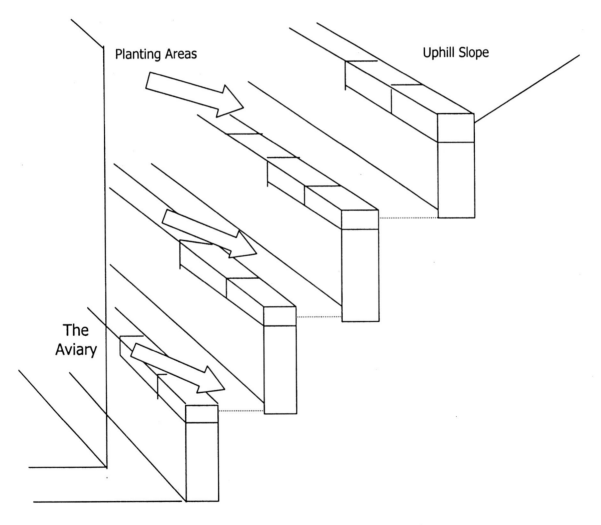

Diagram of Stairstep Terracing

The lower level of the terrace is far less likely to cause similar problems. Usually, simply covering the bare ground of the slope below the aviary with a heavy layer of organic matter will prevent any further sliding or erosion. In areas where pine, fir or spruce trees are in abundance, you can cover the ground with a heavy layer of their needles. In areas of deciduous forest, leaves and leaf mold gathered and spread on the slope will perform the same function. A combination of leaves and needles is best.

If trees are scarce where you have built your aviary, buy a few bales of hay and scatter the hay heavily on the slope. This will stabilize the slope during rains and heavy snowfall. Also, the native grass and plant seeds that are found in any soil will sprout during the growing season to further stabilize and solidify the lower slope. Gradually, the organic matter will decompose, at which time you may need to add more. More often, the native plants have already taken over the slope and will keep it stable. If native growth is insufficient to do the job satisfactorily, you may have to scatter some grass seed and clover seed, raking it into the soil and keeping it watered to sprout, grow and stabilize the lower slope. In desert areas, you can use cactus, sage, and a large variety of other hardy, desert plants to stabilize the lower slope. In the few areas that are too dry for any permanent plant growth other than annual plants that are reseeded, you can simply stack rocks on the slope to keep the soil from shifting and being eroded by winds or rains.

For the slopes on either side of the aviary that are on the same level as the aviary, first a little work with hand tools to gentle the slopes will be necessary. Once the angle of the slope is worked to the point where it is no steeper than about thirty degrees, you can proceed to cover the slope with organic matter and native plants for permanent stability, as I have recommended for the lower slope. Again in extremely dry areas, you can always find rocks to pile on the slope that will prevent the soil from eroding. In mild climates where freezes are unknown, a huge variety of native cactus and succulents are available that will enable you to create an attractive and beautiful, rocky, landscaped slope on the lower side of your aviary.

In areas where temperatures go far below freezing and winter snows are common, there are still varieties of cactus and succulents that you can use for this purpose. These plants are native to the dry, cold, western areas of the United States, and are available from nurseries that specialize in these types of vegetation. A few cactus species in the genera *Echinocereus* and *Escobaria* are cold hardy, and there are also at least two species of *Agave* and numerous succulents and hardy desert flowers that you can use to stabilize the slopes around your dry country aviary. All of these cold-hardy, desert plants are available from High Country Gardens, 2902 Rufina Street, Santa Fe, New Mexico 87507-2929.

If your terracing is on a shaded slope, each terrace will look very attractive when planted with various ferns and impatiens. These plants do well in any shady location, so long as the shade continues through the hottest portions or the day. Early morning and late afternoon sun will be all right, however, and sunlight at these times will give the shade loving plants all of the light that they need for normal growth and blooming for the impatiens.

Once all four sloping areas of your terracing are permanently stabilized, you can proceed to build your aviary on the flat space you have provided with no danger of later damage from landslide or erosion. Though the site preparation for an aviary of this type on a terraced slope is very time consuming and intensive, once the preparation is completed, the construction of the aviary itself will be no more difficult that it would have been on a completely flat location.

After thoroughly examining the proposed location for your aviary, if you decide to build and blend the aviary into the slope, you will not need the extensive preparation work that is involved in the terracing method discussed above. However, you will still need to have a flat area at both the upper and lower slope that is wide enough to permit you to place a ladder that will be steady and safe for working on the top of the aviary. Do not neglect this flat area at both the top and bottom of the sloping aviary, or you will regret it at a later date when you need to perform some work on the top of the aviary.

When you build on a slope, most of the angles you create on at least two sides of the aviary will not be square, ninety degree angles. The actual aviary angles will correspond to the sloping angle of the land. Though the appearance will be very attractive when the aviary is completed, cutting the framing at the correct angle and then fastening the framing securely will take far longer than the time required on an aviary that has all corners squared off.

You can make cutting your framing and hardware cloth to fit the angle of your hill much simpler and more accurate by using a small contractor's aluminum rafter angle square. This handy square will save you hours of time and effort as you cut the angles for the framing of your aviary. It is not expensive and will last for many years for any subsequent work you may be doing in framing or cutting. I used one for over 20 years before finally losing it somewhere so that I was forced to buy another.

Depending on how you overlap or join the framing, you may be able to fasten some of the framing with galvanized nails, which are always the cheapest and best method of fastening aviary framing. If the angle for joining the framing cannot be fastened securely with nails, it will be best to use the preformed galvanized metal fasteners to join the framing, nailing them in place with the 1½ inch galvanized roofing nails. These fasteners have predrilled holes that make nailing fast and create a secure frame joint wherever they have to be used.

Another requirement that will be vital for the entire life of the aviary is the requirement to build solid terracing on the inside of the aviary. All birds with their incessant activity will constantly be pushing dirt towards the lower side of the sloping aviary. With finches, this may take several years to become a serious problem. With pheasants, quail, or other gallinaceous birds, a couple of weeks on a slope will have them on the verge of digging their way out of the aviary, if you have left the sloping interior intact. Even the larger doves and pigeons will move enough soil in their normal eating and foraging activities in a sloping aviary so that the dirt rapidly will begin to accumulate on the lower side of the aviary.

Your interior terracing can be formal with bricks, pressure treated wood or blocks, or you can use the native rocks to create a free-form, natural appearing series of interior terraces in the aviary. Build a larger terrace at the location where you intend to put the food and water containers, as this is the most likely area for the birds to be scratching around. With several of these terraces installed, dirt flowing down the hillside will be minimal and controlled. Without this preplanning and terracing, you will surely constantly be forced to push or carry soil from the lower part of the aviary to the higher part.

Plants and grass placed on each terrace will help to hold the soil while the birds in the aviary engage in their normal eating and foraging. The variety of plants and grass you can use will vary with each climate area, of course, and all of this information will be covered in detail in Chapter 11.

Whether your aviary is built on a terrace or built at an angle to conform to the slope of the hillside, you must still have a level area in front of your aviary door to permit easy access to the aviary. Starting where the door is hinged, the level area should extend out for the width of the door and then for an additional three feet in order to give you room to move around the open door. The level area should also extend at least three feet beyond the door on the side that opens to allow you to enter and leave the aviary easily and safely in all weather conditions. A slope of any kind in front of the aviary door is an invitation for disaster, particularly when the ground becomes covered with snow and ice in the winter.

Even in areas that get no snow or freezing temperatures, rain and the resulting mud on a slope will make that slope very slippery, indeed. In areas of snow and ice, the slightest slope will become icy and will make your access to the aviary next to impossible. At best, a slippery slope in front of an aviary door will cause you to slip and fall, spilling any food you may be carrying for the aviary. At worst, you will fall and tear the door of the aviary off of its hinges catching yourself, or you will break bones that will result in a long and painful recovery. Be sure that the area in front of your aviary door is level and covered with a non-slippery material for safety. Gravel is one of the better ground coverings in front of the door of the aviary.

I have also used pine needles quite effectively and successfully in front of aviary doors, though pine needles can become slippery when they become wet. A thick layer of straw, hay, or dead leaves can also serve the purpose efficiently. Any of the organic materials that you use in front of the aviary door have the noticeable advantage of constant decomposition, mainly caused by all of the bacteria and other microorganisms in the soil. Decomposition creates heat. This means that snow and ice that falls or forms on this thick layer of organic matter will thaw far faster than snow or ice that covers bare, frozen soil.

Chapter 8

Heating the Aviary

Unless you live in Hawaii or Puerto Rico, auxiliary heat will at some point become needed in the aviary in order to keep the birds healthy during periods of colder weather. Most areas in the United States and all areas in Canada will need heat of some kind during at least six months of the year. Still, your object must not be to keep your aviary birds in a hothouse environment. All healthy birds, even the most tropical species, should be able to tolerate temperatures down to the freezing point with no undue discomfort and remain in perfect health. However, for those birds from south of the Equator that breeding primarily during our fall and winter months in North America, the night temperatures should not go below 50 degrees Fahrenheit. Birds that do not brood their young after they reach a week or so of age should be kept in a much warmer environment. Otherwise, you will lose the babies on cool nights before the nestlings are able to control their own body temperatures.

One of the most serious problems that any breeder or fancier will encounter occasionally is the extreme temperature sensitivity of those birds that people have raised or maintained for a long period of time in an overly warm environment and hothouse conditions. By overly warm, I mean any temperatures that are consistently maintained over 75° Fahrenheit or 24° Centigrade. Perhaps the worst conditions are those in which the temperature in the birds' area is thermostatically controlled and never varies. Once the birds adapt their bodies and their metabolism to a steady temperature of 85° Fahrenheit, for example, any sudden lowering of the temperature is likely to kill them.

Breeders who keep all of their finches at a standard hothouse environmental temperature of 80° are taking a terrible gamble. Particularly in cold climates, an unexpected cold snap and power failure may cut off all heat for many hours, even days. I have found from experience that even wood stoves that are designed to operate with an electric blower will produce only 25% to 50% of their normal heat output when the power to the fan system is off. If the temperature in your bird room falls from a steady 80° Fahrenheit to a cooler 60° during a power failure, you can expect to lose over half of your birds. Should the temperature fall to 50° Fahrenheit or less, you will probably lose them all. Birds that are maintained at a constant warm temperature simply cannot adjust and control their body temperatures when the temperature in their birdroom suddenly drops from a steady 85° Fahrenheit down to 60°. Their body temperature will fall below the minimum necessary for their lives, and they will die.

The reason for this sensitivity is easy to explain. The bird's body allocates the energy from the food it consumes to allow muscular exercise for flight, walking, displaying, and other normal physical functions, and also for the maintenance of the body's normal temperature. Since a bird's normal body temperature is well over 100° Fahrenheit, a high surrounding air temperature will mean that the bird's body allocates far less energy to heat production. When the heat requirement skyrockets without warning as air temperature plummets, a bird will be unable to adjust its metabolism rapidly enough to compensate for the radical drop in the temperature of its local environment. As a result, its body temperature falls, it puffs up its feathers to conserve body heat, and it becomes lethargic. If the body temperature falls below a certain point, bodily functions cease, and the bird dies.

The human metabolism works similarly. In Miami, the overcoats come out of the closet when the temperature goes down to 60°, while in Fairbanks, Alaska, a spring temperature that rises to 45° Fahrenheit brings everyone out in short sleeves to enjoy the nice weather after a long, cold winter.

I once obtained a pair of Gouldian finches that had been raised and maintained under a controlled temperature of 75° Fahrenheit. They were gorgeous birds and were in perfect health for several months of the summer. However, when autumn arrived and the night temperature in my birdroom went down to 60° for the first time, both of these Gouldians fell off of the perch dead during the night. None of my other Gouldians nor any of the other 400 or so birds in the same area were affected in the least. That was a very painful, but also a very valuable lesson, and similar experiences on more than one occasion have resulted in the advice presented in this chapter.

The Gouldian Finches that I kept recently have been conditioned to tolerate temperatures that were considerably below freezing. At my location in the North Carolina mountains at one time, any windstorm or snowstorm might mean an extended power failure. At one point, my power was off for a full five days. During one power outage that lasted two days, the temperatures outside dipped below 15° Fahrenheit. Even inside, the Gouldians were used to night temperatures that dipped to 40°, so they came though this cold spell with no heat in perfect condition. My Gouldians spent one winter outdoors with the night temperatures often in the teens and dipping as low as 9° Fahrenheit. Their water containers were frozen solid and had to be thawed with warm water three times a day so the birds could drink. Any bird that was accustomed to 'hothouse' conditions would never have been able to survive conditions this severe.

You should also be aware that many of our common finch species are not good brooders of their young. The Lady Gouldian Finches are a perfect example of this, and even a dedicated breeding pair will cease brooding their young when they are about a week old. Should the temperature at this point go below about 70° Fahrenheit, the unbrooded babies in the nest through the night will die of exposure. These babies are unable to regulate their own body heat adequately until they begin to feather out. Though Zebra Finches and Society Finches are much better at brooding their young, when the night temperatures go below freezing, even these species may not be able to keep their babies warm enough through the night to prevent them from dying.

When you plan for the heating of an aviary, plan for conditions within the aviary to remain well above freezing, but do not plan on keeping your aviary at the temperature you would expect in your living room, unless you are breeding the species that are poor brooders of their young. This high temperature is not only unnecessary, it is foolish. Nature has prepared the birds to tolerate rapid and extreme changes in weather conditions and still remain in perfect health. You need to allow those same conditions to remain in effect in your outdoor aviary. Heating in an aviary is only to keep the birds from suffering when your outdoor temperatures go far below freezing in the winter. No auxiliary heat should ever be necessary for nights that dip only into the forties and fifties on the Fahrenheit thermometer, again unless you are raising the species that breed during our fall and winter, and that are such poor night brooders of their young.

With this background in mind for the birds' requirements, the next information you need is a short lesson in the physical properties of heat. Since heat is an increase in the movement or vibrations of the molecules of a substance, any liquid or gas that will circulate can be used to transfer heat. Air and water are the two substances most commonly used to transfer heat from one location to another. However, water has two characteristics that can cause severe problems in a circulating system. Water freezes at 32° Fahrenheit or 0° Centigrade, and it will boil at a fairly low temperature in a heating system. For these reasons, either an antifreeze solution or an oil solution that will not freeze or boil readily is most frequently used to transfer heat in a circulating system.

Second, heat rises. This simple, basic fact of our physical world is ignored more often than any other natural law in human designing and construction. This requirement for heated gases and liquids to rise means that any heated air or water will rise as far as it can in your home or in an aviary. This is why the outlet of your electric or gas water heater is on the top of the tank. The heating elements are at the mid-point or the low-point of the water heater. This is why heating elements for rooms are at the base of the walls, rather than at the ceiling, and also why heating vents are most often located on the floor of the house. Heating by means of radiant ceilings is a very inefficient heating method for any home or building.

When we apply these laws to the outdoor aviary, we must first be sure that the aviary will hold any heat that is generated or produced. Particularly in the colder climates, some type of insulation may be necessary to hold the heat in the aviary and to minimize the loss and waste of the energy that provides the heat. In harsher climates, an area of the aviary that is almost completely enclosed and heated is almost a necessity. The entrance for the birds should be at the lower level of the enclosure. Little heat will be lost through a lower access entrance for the birds of this type.

There are a number of different types of heating systems that you can use in an enclosed aviary. Each of these has its advantages and disadvantages, of course, and you will need to look at each type closely to decide which will be best for your location and climate and for the aviary you are heating.

If you live in an area that has dependable sunshine during the months of the winter, the cleanest and least expensive way to heat your aviary is by using the sun. Particularly if your aviary is placed on a southern slope with no trees, hills, buildings or mountains to block the sunlight, this can be an easy and effective way to heat your aviary during the colder months. An area of the aviary covered with clear fiberglass or polycarbonate sheeting will allow the sun's rays to pass through and heat the interior of the aviary.

If you have installed a dark or flat black surface to receive the sunlight, this will act almost like a heating element. Visible light rays striking this dark surface are reflected at the longer infrared wavelengths of heat and will rapidly warm the interior. The same process is at work on a cold day when your vehicle warms up nicely from the sunlight shining through the windows. Even on cloudy days you will still receive some warming effect from the limited light rays that are reflected as heat from any dark surface. However, if you live in a climate that is cloudy for most of the days of the winter, you would be wise to plan on an alternate method of heating for your aviary. Several other possible methods are also covered in this chapter.

Using solar panels is another possibility for heating your aviary, though the expense of the initial installation of the solar panels makes this method somewhat impractical for this purpose. Again, for this type of heating, a southern exposure for your aviary is best, an exposure that is free of any obstruction that would block the sunlight for part of the day. A solar panel placed below the aviary that heats an antifreeze liquid and allows the heated liquid to circulate upward into the aviary is the most efficient way for making use of the solar panels for heating your aviary.

Electric heating for your aviary will, of course, be the cleanest, but probably not the cheapest form of aviary heat. Also, with electric heat, there are no fumes to concern you when heating an aviary for the birds, and you can use the heat from an electric heater directly in the aviary without worrying about smoke or fumes poisoning the birds. After due consideration, should you decide that the ease of installation and maintenance free operation of electric heating are the most important factors for your aviary, an electric heater is a logical method for warming the air in the aviary to a point comfortable for the birds. The use of electric heat requires that you have an enclosed and insulated aviary space, of course, or much of your heat and the money to purchase it will be wasted.

The standard space heaters and baseboard heaters that are used in the home are not the best for the aviary, as they become too hot, and even when protected may cause injury to one or more of your birds, particularly the fledglings. Fledglings have little or no control over their flying, and they may stay on a surface that is too hot for their comfort long enough to cause injury or death.

The best type of electric heater for this purpose is the one that is shaped like one of the radiators that would be used for steam heat. These are filled with a special kind of oil, and the electric element within the heater heats the oil. The heated oil then circulates around the radiator, warming all of the vanes of the radiator. As the name of this type of heater implies, a radiator radiates heat which is taken from the liquid that flows through the radiator and warms the air that passes through the radiator vanes. Many of the models available are not too hot to touch, but they still allow the flowing air to become warm as it contacts the surface of the radiator.

This air warmed by the radiating heater then rises to warm the interior of the aviary, and cooler air from the lower portions of the aviary continually circulates to the lower point of the radiator, and the cooler air is then drawn through the radiator. This type of electric heater makes good use of the basic principle that heat rises. Most of the radiant heaters of this type also have a variety of heat settings that you can use, depending on how cold the temperatures outside are expected to be. The one I have, for example, has a setting for 600 watts when less heat is needed, a 900 watt setting for medium heat output, and a 1500 watt setting for the high heat output that your aviary would need on the coldest nights. In addition, this type of heater will be the safest for your birds.

Regardless of whether you use electric heat as your primary heat source or as a backup, you must keep in mind that the supply of electricity is the only one of the heating possibilities that you personally have no control over. Though the supply of electricity from the major suppliers throughout the country is in general distributed very dependably and priced very reasonably, occasional power failures are a fact of life. These power failures can and will occur for a variety of reasons, ranging from system overload or lightning striking a transformer to a tree falling on the power line. You have no control over power failures and you will simply have to wait until the power crews can get the distribution of electricity restored to your home and aviary.

Should you have no backup heat source when one of these power failures occurs, you will lose birds when the temperature in the aviary drops to a low point that is below what the birds within can tolerate. Though in most power failures the electricity is restored within a matter of hours, I previously noted the period when I lived in the mountains of North Carolina. A bad storm caused a power failure so extensive and with so many causes that crews had to work for days to get all of the customers back on line. For us, this power failure lasted for a full five days. No birds that are used to warm and heated conditions will be able to survive an extended period of time such as this without some type of auxiliary heat.

For this reason, it might be best to use a different form of heat generation that you can control as your primary heat source. This would let you use the electric heat as a backup for use only when the primary form of heat generation is temporarily unavailable.

Many areas in the United States offer natural gas as an energy source. Where natural gas is available, heaters are also always available to utilize the natural gas as a source of heat. If you have this option in your area, check with your local gas company to see which types of heaters are available. Once you learn this, you can decide which type would do the best job for you for heating an outdoor aviary.

Though in theory, natural gas burns cleanly and is non-polluting, there are often impurities in any natural gas, including the distinctively odorous compound that is added to the gas to warn when leaks and breaks in the line occur. Pure natural gas has no odor. For this reason, I do not recommend venting a natural gas heater directly into an aviary. It will be far better to use the natural gas heater to heat an antifreeze compound that will circulate into the aviary and will carry the heat with it. The line that carries the antifreeze will transfer the heat into the air in the aviary, then if all has been planned correctly, the cooling liquid will return to the natural gas heater to have its temperature raised again for recirculation.

The comments concerning the natural gas heater will also apply to any propane heater that you might decide to use to heat your aviary. Heating with propane is not cheap, but propane is capable of supplying a huge amount of heat in a hurry, should you decide to use it as a backup. The canisters of propane are available anywhere that items for camping equipment or construction equipment are sold. Contractors use this form of heat frequently for rapidly heating work areas in the winter to make them more comfortable for the construction workers.

Another possibility for heating your aviary is with the use of fuel oil. Again, as with the natural gas and propane heat sources, you will need to set up a circulating system to transfer heat from the heater itself to a circulating antifreeze solution that will heat the aviary. The fumes from burning fuel oil are dangerous to the birds, so a fuel oil heater should not be in the aviary with the birds. Still, fuel oil is widely used and available in most locations in the United States. Also, fuel oil is a concentrated form of natural storage for a huge amount of heat energy.

Heating with coal is another possibility to consider, especially if you live in or near a coal mining area. With little or no shipping to pay for, you can probably pick up coal for a very reasonable price at the mining area. This is particularly true if you can use the lower grades of coal that are available at a much reduced price. If you have a good source for coal at a reasonable price, this can be a logical fuel to use for the heating of your outdoor aviary.

As you consider the possibility of coal for heating, you also need to be aware that the fumes from burning coal carry a variety of elements and compounds that are inimical to the health of the birds. Any use of coal in a small stove will also cause the coal to burn less efficiently and consequently will create more pollutants in the smoke and fumes released from the burning coal.

For these reasons, if you decide to use coal for heating your outdoor aviary, you will have to use an indirect system, as I recommended for the natural gas, propane, and fuel oil heating possibilities. The coal stove would heat a closed system of circulating antifreeze liquid to transfer the heat from the stove into the aviary itself. As the liquid circulates through the aviary, it will cool off and then return to the stove for reheating.

All of these fuels discussed up to this point are generally referred to as fossil fuels, as they seem to be the result of the decomposition of rampant ancient life forms. As such, these fuels are not renewable in the current era, and once they are used, they are gone and are irreplaceable. As the more easily available deposits of these fossil fuels are used up, they will become harder to find, harder to extract, and therefore more expensive.

In many areas, wood is an alternate heat source that you should seriously consider. Wood is the only heating method other than solar energy that is a renewable resource. All of the other gas, coal, and oil heat sources are finite in quantity on the earth, and once used, they are gone. A stand of growing trees, however, will continue to produce dead wood for burning and heating as long as the climate stays relatively stable and the sun continues to shine.

The sources of wood for use as a fuel are found in all areas except the driest deserts or in the coldest arctic areas. If you have to buy the wood for your heating, however, using wood to heat your aviary will not be economical. Still, if you have a small woodlot or live next to a state or national forest area, you will have a readily available source for dry, dead wood that is an ideal fuel for supplying an aviary heating system. You can often get a limited permit from the forest rangers in charge of the area near you to gather deadfall to fuel your wood stove at no charge.

As a fuel, wood has many of the disadvantages that are also inherent in gas, oil and coal. Burning wood gives off fumes and smoke that will be harmful to birds in the aviary, so a system of circulating antifreeze solution will also be necessary for a wood heat source. The cost of setting up the circulating system will be similar to that discussed for the fossil fuels.

In addition, a wood stove will be necessary. Though these are widely available and not overly expensive, they are quite heavy. They will be difficult to handle and difficult to install. Nevertheless, with a free source of wood for heating your aviary, a wood stove with the accompanying circulating system for the heating liquid may be a very worthwhile investment.

For those who have wood freely available and choose to use wood as a fuel for heating their aviary, a few other comments are in order. Green wood that has not had years to dry out thoroughly still contains a large percentage of water. For this reason, it will burn slowly and poorly with an excess of smoke and a minimum of heat. Green wood is not a satisfactory fuel for use in a wood stove, except in emergency.

The best wood for use as a fuel is a dry hardwood. Examples of native North American wood trees that are considered to be hardwoods are the oaks, hickories, maples and walnuts. This type of wood is harder, denser, and burns the longest. The hardwoods will be the cleanest types of wood to use as a fuel in a wood stove.

Softwoods are less dense and burn faster. Some examples of common North American softwoods are pine, fir, spruce, cedar and poplar. They frequently contain resins that burn incompletely in the relatively low heat of a wood stove. As a result of this incomplete combustion, softwoods can create deposits of creosote in the stovepipe and chimney. Should the creosote become hot enough to catch fire at a later time, it will create a chimney fire hot enough to melt the stovepipe.

Though you also can use charcoal as a fuel for heating the circulating liquid for warming your aviary, charcoal has the same advantages and disadvantages that you will find in wood when you use it as a fuel. Charcoal is, after all, partially burned wood that has been compressed into a more compact and cleaner burning form. For most aviculturists, charcoal will not be a serious possibility for use as a fuel for heating an outdoor aviary. Unless you have a very dependable source of charcoal for free or at a very reasonable price, you are much farther ahead to use the available sources of wood as your primary fuel.

The establishment of a closed system for circulating antifreeze from a heating unit to the aviary as discussed with most of the sources of heat, of course, requires a considerable initial investment. The pipes, connectors, antifreeze solution, insulating covering and the installation of all of this requires a lot of time and effort, also. However, in those areas where one of these fuels is cheap and readily available, it is often economical to put more into the initial system and pay less for the fuel itself whenever it is needed. You will need to study what is available in your local area in the way of heat sources before you make a final decision on your heat source or begin the construction of the circulating antifreeze system.

Regardless of which type of heat you eventually decide to use for your outdoor aviary, be aware that any heating method which utilizes burning material must be carefully shielded from the birds. Nothing will panic your birds worse than a visible fire. Nature has equipped these birds with an instinctive fear of fire, and even the smallest flame will send an entire aviary into panic.

At one time, I maintained about eighty cages of birds in a separate birdroom. Though this aviary was separated from the rest of the house by two walls, it was still possible to hear the birds from the main house and to note anything unusual in their sound or behavior. One evening, after all of the lights were out, I heard the birdroom erupt in total panic. When I opened the door to check on the birds, I noted that a coupling in an electrical cord had overheated and that a small flame was burning the plastic connector. Though this flame was no more than one inch high, it was still sufficient to panic every bird in the birdroom. All birds will panic instinctively even in the presence of so small a flame.

Each aviculturist's conditions are different and most are unique. Thus, no recommendation or statement can be 100% true for all times and conditions. With all of the heating possibilities before you, you alone will have to decide which will be best for your location, your environment and your local conditions. Your access to unusual fuels that are available free of charge may make those fuels become a serious possibility for the heating of your outdoor aviary.

As an example of this type of specialized item available to very few, but still available free of charge, I recall reading a question on canaries many years ago. Most breeders would never consider feeding walnuts to their canaries, because they are simply too expensive for this purpose. However, this breeder lived in a walnut grove and was feeding the walnuts regularly to her canaries, who loved them. She wanted to be sure that this was an acceptable food for her canaries. Absolutely and positively -- walnuts are a very nutritious food, very low in water content, and are a far better food for canaries than hemp seed, for example, which has been heated and treated to kill the viability of the hemp seed. Though walnuts may not be a normal food that canary breeders offer to their canaries, still you can be certain that walnuts are an excellent food for the canaries, especially when they are free!

Chapter 9

Locations for Food, Perches and Water

The placing and location of the food, perches and water in an aviary is crucial to the health and safety of the birds in any outdoor aviary. Simply placing these items haphazardly with no planning will result in a host of later problems and frustrations that you could easily have prevented with a little forethought. Over the years, I have noted a wide variety of types of feeding stations, feeding methods, perches available, and water systems at a variety of outdoor aviaries. All of the different methods used in providing these necessities get the job done -- the birds get fed, they have a place to perch, and they have water. However, there ways to supply these necessities that are easier and safer than others. The object of this chapter is to outline the best ways to provide the food, water and perches in an aviary. Then, you can choose the method that will work best for your conditions.

FOOD DISHES AND LOCATION

The most successful feeding location that I have used for birds in an outdoor aviary consisted of a simple treated fence post placed upright near the center of their outdoor aviary in an area that is covered and protected from rain and snow. Place a flat board or piece of plywood on top of this pole to create a platform. A good size for this platform is about 18 inches by 18 inches. A lip added on all sides of this platform that is about three-quarters of an inch high will hold most of the seed and the other food items on the platform as the birds scatter it around in their normal eating and foraging activities.

This upright pole with its feeding platform up near the top of the aviary under the covering will stay reasonably dry even during periods of windy, blowing rain. On the rare days that you get a rain that goes sideways to such an extent that it soaks the feeding platform, you can clean out the wet food from the feeding platform and then just scatter it on the ground. The ground dwelling birds and the other birds in the aviary will still eat most of the wet food, and any that is not eaten will be mixed with the soil and composted along with the birds' droppings. Birds actually prefer to eat their food off of the ground, if you can give them that choice.

On normal sunny or cloudy days, the seeds and other food items that the birds will still fling out of this high platform will fall on the ground and will provide plenty of available food for the ground dwelling birds in the aviary, such as the small doves and quail. When this platform on a pole is placed away from the outer walls of the aviary, this type of feeding station also will prevent predators or visitors outside the aviary from frightening the birds away from the food while they are eating.

Alternately, you can place the food in dishes or containers on the ground under the covered area of the aviary. The worst disadvantage in placing the feed dishes in this location is that a driving rain can soak all of the food in the dish. However, though the food containers in this location are far more likely to get wet when a rainstorm blows the rainwater sideways, they will still be useful for the gentle rainy or drizzly days that you get periodically without any strong winds. Once a storm is past, you can easily scatter any of the food that gets wet, and the birds still will eat most of it on the ground. Experience has taught, also, that birds of all kinds seem to prefer to eat their food off of the ground. I have had finches refuse to eat their normal foods when they were placed on concrete. Once the food was moved onto an area of soil, they ate the food readily.

After trying a wide variety of food containers over the years in a variety of outdoor aviaries, I have settled on the use of the standard ceramic feeding dishes that are normally used for dogs and cats. These ceramic dishes are impervious to water, droppings, mud, broken eggs or any other substance that gets on them. If washed while the dirt is still damp, cleaning them is a five second job. Even if the dirt has hardened onto the ceramic, a very short soak in water will allow you to clean the ceramic dishes easily and completely. Though the ceramic dishes will break, under normal aviary use they are permanent and untarnishable. But yes, I have had large birds break one of these ceramic dishes by moving the ceramic dish so that it dropped on a rock.

Plastic dishes of any type are unsatisfactory over the long haul. Any dishes made of plastic scratch easily, and they are very difficult to clean once they are fouled with droppings or dried food products. In time, the plastic material becomes brittle and will crack. Also, dirt, food particles and droppings collect in the scratches in the plastic, and the plastic feeding dishes do not look clean no matter how long you soak them and scrub them.

You can also buy feeding dishes that are made of glass, though this type is harder to find. Alternately, you can buy glass dishes that are meant for human food use in any large variety store. Glass dishes have the distinct advantage that they are very easy to keep clean. Like the ceramic dishes, however, glass feeding dishes are breakable.

Another type of feeding dish that most farm stores, pet shops and variety stores carry is the type that is made of stainless steel. Most of these stainless steel dishes are of one piece construction, and they have no seams that will collect dirt and droppings or that will harbor harmful microorganisms. Like the glass and ceramic feeding dishes, the stainless steel dishes are fairly easy to clean. As the birds we raise are not the cleanest little creatures in the world, dishes that are easily cleaned are always of positive advantage in the outdoor aviary.

The easiest types of feeders to use for seed are those types that screw onto a standard quart canning jar. Several styles of these feeder bases are available in both metal and plastic. They have at least two notable advantages, also. First, you can see the level of seed in the jar at a glance, and easily refill the jar when the level becomes too low and the birds are running out of seed. The birds rapidly learn that pecking at the jar itself gets them no seed, and they also learn that the seed comes from the base of the container. Also, if a driving rain soaks the seed in one of these containers, only the seed that has flowed out into the base will be wet. The seed remaining in the canning jar is still dry, so resetting the feeder is simplicity itself.

PERCHES AND LOCATION

Birds will perch on anything in the aviary, and are perfectly happy to hang onto the wire or hardware cloth on the sides of the aviary. The birds are completely capable of living out their lives in an aviary that has no perches at all, and in which the nesting sites are fastened to the sides of the aviary. Nevertheless, birds hanging onto the aviary wire are an invitation to predators, and any nesting sites on the sides of the aviary will be certain to result in night panics and abandoned nests as predators climb up the aviary wire and panic the birds off of their nests. Several places in this book I have stressed that you not place either perches or nesting sites on the sides of the aviary or even close to the hardware cloth, and again I stress this as the cause of many aviary breeding failures.

The best types of perches for any aviary are those formed by natural trees and bushes that are planted in the aviary. In a newly planted or sparsely planted aviary, however, additional perching areas may be advisable. In this case, I recommend again the placing of a treated fence post in the aviary, with one end buried far enough so that the pole will be stable in any wind or through any actions of the birds. To this pole you should attach the springy natural branches that will serve as the perches. This is also a good location for attaching nesting sites for the birds.

The worst type of perches for any birds are the wooden dowel rods that come as standard perches in all of the small cages and flight cages that are sold. These are slippery, and they offer no variation in angle, texture, or size for the birds' feet. The feet need these differing sizes and varying textures whenever the birds land in order to exercise their muscles and tendons properly. The leg muscles and their tendons also need the varying angles of natural perches for getting their proper exercise. If you have to use a cage with the dowels installed, remove them and replace them with natural rough branches that you have cut from a shrub, bush or tree. Even in a densely populated city location, people are always trimming bushes and trees, and will be happy to give you a few of these branches for bird perches. Very few areas are left in our cities that are completely stone and concrete. People have come to recognize the importance of living plants and trees around their living and work areas, and most new buildings are now designed to allow for at least a minimal amount of plantings and landscaping

As I have repeatedly stressed, any perches that you place in the aviary should be away from the sides of the aviary. Though attaching the perches to a pole placed in the ground is the most satisfactory, you can also attach the perches to the roof framing of the aviary where the framing is under cover and safe from predator attack. When you place perches too close to the sides of the aviary, any predator climbing up the wire at night will panic the birds. Night panics are largely preventable, and preventing them should be one of the very highest priorities in the planning and building of your outdoor aviary.

For any aviary in any climate, remember that the highest perches in the aviary should be under the covering. Refer to the discussion of open and covered areas in Chapter 12 for more complete information on the covered and enclosed areas for an outdoor aviary. The highest perches are where the non-breeding birds will roost for the night, and it is also the area where the mates for brooding birds will sleep every night. It is vital that these high perches are in a dry area that will not be completely soaked by even a gusting, windy, rainy night. In cold climates, the highest perches should be in your enclosed area so that the birds are safe from outside predators and also somewhat protected from the coldest air, even if the aviary is unheated.

WATER CONTAINERS AND LOCATION

Water is a vital necessity for all of your birds, and there are a variety of ways to provide water to your birds. A bewildering variety of drinkers, fountains, dishes and containers are advertised on the market exclusively for birds. Many of the pet waterers and water containers on the market that are designed for dogs, cats, rabbits, guinea pigs or other small animals are also easily adaptable for providing a constant supply of water to your birds.

Your local conditions, the placing of your aviary, and the availability of water will all affect your final decision as to the type of water container you will use in your outdoor aviary. I will cover in general the types of containers on the market that are available for your use, outline the advantages and disadvantages of each type, and then provide the benefit of my own experience in providing water for birds in outdoor aviaries to advise you of my own personal preferences.

The plastic water containers are made in many styles and types, and they have the decided advantage of being the cheapest water containers that are available on the market. They also have the previously noted disadvantages of plastic -- it will scratch easily and will be very difficult to keep clean. Dirt and microorganisms will be nearly impossible to get out of these scratched areas, and they will be a constant source of contamination for the water in the plastic container. In time, the plastic will crack and disintegrate, particularly if you have placed the container in a sunny location. Should the water freeze in a plastic container, the water will expand as ice, and it will crack the container badly enough that it will no longer hold water. For these reasons, I only use plastic containers as a stopgap measure and a temporary solution.

Glass containers for water are about the easiest to clean and to keep clean water available to the birds. A glass waterer will not scratch, and when the birds foul it with food particles and droppings, glass is very easy to wash or wipe clean. Glass will not harbor microorganisms, and the very worst you can expect in the way of contamination is that algae will occasionally grow on the damp glass. The algae cells are always present in the air, and when they fall on damp glass, this provides ideal conditions for the algae to live, grow and multiply. This is not necessarily bad, and I have known canary breeders who would not clean out their glass waterers that were green with algae, as they viewed the algae as a very positive addition to the birds' daily diet.

Glass containers have only a couple of disadvantages, but those disadvantages are severe. Glass breaks easily, and in any situation where the glass may be dropped or slid into a rock, for example, it will break. Equally bad, if an unexpected cold spell should freeze the water in a glass water container, the container will crack and break from the pressure of the expanding ice. If you live in a cooler climate that is subject to unexpected freezes that are not in the weather forecast, do not use glass waterers. Even though science classifies glass technically as a supercooled liquid rather than as a true solid, it certainly is the most brittle and breakable liquid known.

Ceramic containers as a class are very similar to glass containers with the same advantages and disadvantages. Whereas glass containers for pet watering are very difficult to find, except for the types of waterers made of other materials that use a standard glass canning jar, the ceramic containers are available everywhere, and they are one of the commonest types used. As food containers, I consider them the best type that is available. As water containers, however, like the glass containers, they are too brittle to trust to an unexpected freeze.

Several types of metal watering containers are also on the market. Primary among these are the types of galvanized steel water containers that are designed and used for farms and poultry. The main advantages to these waterers is their easy availability at any farm or feed store, and their relatively inexpensive price. Also, for colder climates, there are electric heating elements made for placing under these galvanized containers that will provide them with a constant low heat and will prevent them from freezing. Most farm stores in the colder climates also carry those heating elements in stock. After using them for over two years, they have proven to be very effective in below freezing temperatures.

As disadvantages, these poultry waterers are subject to rust when the combined corrosive effects of the birds' droppings and scattered food particles neutralize and dissolve the galvanizing (zinc coating) to leave the steel bare and unprotected. Also, should an unexpected hard freeze occur, without an automatic heating element, the pressure of the ice within the galvanized containers will separate the container at the seams and make it useless.

If there is no possibility of electrical energy for the aviary, there is still a very effective way of providing a constant supply of water for all of the birds that are in the aviary. Stainless steel water dishes are the type that are needed for this application. A number of differently sized stainless steel dishes are now manufactured for the huge industry that supplies feeding supplies for cats and dogs. These stainless steel dishes range from very small ones that will hold less than half a pint to those meant for large dogs that will hold up to two quarts of food or water. Though all of the sizes are readily available, you may have to search around in your own area to find them, as most stores carry only the plastic and ceramic types. Farm stores and pet shops often carry them, and the large variety stores may also carry them in their pet departments.

The advantage to these stainless steel dishes is that the sides are not straight, at a 90° angle, but are beveled so that the base of the dish is quite a bit smaller than the larger top of the dish. As they are one piece construction, with no seams to hold dirt and droppings or to split, they are ideal for bird use in an outdoor aviary, even when the temperatures are going below freezing every night. When you use them outdoors as bird waterers in freezing weather, even if the stainless steel dish freezes solid, it will not split, and it will not be damaged. More likely, the pressure of the ice within the dish will simply pop the ice up and out of the dish. Each morning then, you can remove the ice and add water for the birds. On the days that may stay below freezing throughout the day, you may have to add water for the birds several times.

I have used the smallest size stainless steel cat dish, available at Wal-Mart stores as a standard stock item, for finches in flight cages that are maintained out of doors all through the winter. This stainless steel dish is imported from India, and it serves the purpose of supplying water to the birds in the cages throughout the winter. Though the dish may freeze solid during the night, each morning I only have to remove the ice if the dish is full and then add water. If the dish was only half full, it is a simple job to pour the fresh morning water on top of the ice. In testing dozens of these stainless steel dishes through the winter, none were damaged in the slightest by the alternate freezing and thawing of the water in them. On the worst winter mornings when the temperature is considerably below freezing, holding the frozen dishes in a pail of warm water for a few seconds is sufficient to release the ice in them, and I can then add the fresh water for the birds.

The birds' favorite perching trick, of course, is to perch on the side of the water container, get a drink, and then turn around and deposit a dropping into the water. This occurs several times a day in the behavior of any single bird, and the result at the end of the day in a flight cage containing a dozen birds is a very badly fouled water container. The stainless steel dishes that the birds use in this manner are very easily cleaned. I can recommend the stainless steel dishes for any situation in which you are giving birds water in an outdoor aviary.

Should you have the marvelous advantage of living on a very gentle slope with a clear stream or brook running through it, you have the most desirable area available for building aviaries and then providing them with a constant supply of fresh water.

An area such as this is desirable for many purposes, of course, and in any area of the United States where a site with these advantages becomes available, it is likely to be a very expensive parcel of property.

Alternately, if you have several aviaries, you can run a water line through each one. After using several watering methods over the years, this is the one that I would recommend as the easiest to use and the best for the birds. An underground water line will be the safest, and it will not detract from the appearance of the aviary. Putting the water line underground will prevent damage from any number of sources, and at the same time, burying the line will prevent the line from freezing when the temperature becomes more severe in the winter. At a specified place in each aviary, you can install a faucet. I have used the standard brass outdoor water faucets for this purpose, and have found that they work perfectly. When the water pressure is established, turn each faucet in each aviary on just enough that it will release a steady drip of water.

Place a shallow saucer under each faucet to receive the steady dripping. You can buy small saucers for this purpose very cheaply in any variety store where dishes are sold. The birds in the aviary can get a drink or take a bath in this saucer whenever they feel the need. As the saucer fills and overflows, any droppings, food particles and other impurities that have collected in the saucer gradually wash out and soak into the soil. Each day, as you check the feed, you can simply swish the water and any accumulated dirt out of the saucer and leave the faucet at its normal steady drip. On the unusual days when some really obnoxious mess has lodged in the saucer, you can simply open the faucet for a little stronger water flow to clean it out. Once the saucer is clean again, you can reduce the faucet once again to its steady drip for the day. This is the aviary water supply that I would choose over all others in climates that allow it. Also, this method actually wastes very little water, as the steady dripping only releases a gallon or so of water each day.

OTHER COMMENTS

Acclimating any new birds to your outdoor aviary conditions is often only a matter of controlling the microorganisms they are exposed to and feeding them a balanced diet that is high in complete protein, as well as all of the vital vitamins and minerals that they need. These small birds have very limited body reserves when illness strikes, and for this reason, a sick finch or canary almost invariably dies. Any harmful bacteria that they pick up can infect and shut down their digestive tracts, and these harmful microorganisms will result in any bird's death in short order. The birds must have time to develop an immunity to these harmful bacteria.

You can give them the time they need to develop their immunity to unfamiliar microorganisms by treating their normal drinking water with one drop of a common household sodium hypochlorite bleach to each two or three ounces of water. This will kill all of the harmful microorganisms in the water and in the digestive tract when the birds drink the water, without harming the birds in the least. Use this treatment for three days if some of the birds appear sick, but only for one day as a preventative treatment. The chlorine will kill any bacteria or other microorganisms and will give the bird a chance to develop an immunity to these microorganisms. Birds can develop this immunity from just the presence of dead microorganisms very rapidly. After all, this is the way most human inoculations and vaccines work. Nevertheless, chlorine destroys vitamin E on contact, so don't use any chlorine treatment on a constant basis.

I have found that this simple treatment is nearly 100% effective in preventing sickness in newly acquired birds. In cities where the water supply is already heavily chlorinated, this treatment may not be necessary. Taking finches or canaries for veterinary care, however, is simply never cost effective. The sick bird will be dead before any culture can be made or any effective antibiotic prescribed. Though many individuals in the past have ridiculed this chlorine treatment as at best useless and at worst dangerous to the birds, I feel sure that they haven't even tried this treatment for themselves on birds that were obviously ill. I have used it for many years, and stand solidly behind this recommendation for any new birds that you are adding to your collection. Despite the many aviculturists who are not in favor of this treatment, when you cut down to the bottom line, it is this: the treatment works.

Chapter 10

Nesting Sites for the Aviary

In any natural environment, birds will have a wide variety of possible nesting sites. For most of the birds we keep, these sites may vary from holes in trees to thick bushes and vines, or perhaps the fork of a tree or among clumps of grass. The greater the variety of nesting sites that you offer in your aviaries, the more likely you will be to get successful breeding results. A variety of commercial nest boxes are available for use, but these are not necessarily a prerequisite for successful breeding. Often, the birds will be happy to build their own nest in a hanging basket, a wire container stuffed with hay, a thick bush, small tree or a large clump of grass in the aviary. Even within the same species, mated pairs may choose their nesting sites in very different locations.

As a primary rule for placing nesting receptacles, do not place them directly on the sides of the outdoor aviary. Nests placed on the side of an aviary may be easy to inspect and to install, and, of course, the birds will always use them. However, they are an invitation to disaster on an outdoor aviary. Any climbing predator that is after the birds, particularly at night, will climb the wire and smell the birds within the nest. The predator will then make every effort to get at the nest.

No bird that hears a predator practically on top of it and feels this closeness to a dangerous predator will continue to sit on the nest. The bird will panic and shoot out of the nest like a rocket. In the daytime hours, once a predator has gone, the bird will probably return to the nest to resume its brooding. At night, however, the bird cannot see to return to the nest, and it will not return. By the time daylight comes, the nest will be abandoned.

Before you place your nesting receptacles in the aviary, remember that the birds are most likely to accept a nesting site in an area that the birds consider to be hidden. After all, without a hidden nest, the bird would have no chance to raise young ones in the wild. A nest in plain sight would be an invitation to the first predator that came along to destroy it and eat the eggs or babies within the nest. Even with a well hidden nest, this happens very frequently with wild birds. Remember that the smaller birds and their nests are prey to a large variety of mammals and reptiles. They are also preferred prey for many of the larger birds, such as the jays and raptors. In order to maintain the balance of nature and the balance of the species in nature, a pair of small birds needs to raise only two babies that live to reach adult breeding age and then begin breeding on their own. For every pair of small birds that manages to raise four youngsters to this stage, another pair will be killed and eaten, with no young raised.

In our aviaries, we protect and care for our birds so that the balance of nature is negated. We plan and expect for each pair that we keep to raise twenty, thirty, or even more young ones. When any predator comes upon this bounty of prey and food, it is only natural that they make a very serious attempt to thin out this overpopulation. In a natural situation, the limitation of food alone would prevent this concentration of birds in such a small area. When you look at your outdoor aviary from the eyes of the predators and the requirements of the balance of nature, it is easy to see why we wage a continual battle to protect the birds in our outdoor aviaries from their dangerous enemies.

The most common nesting boxes that are available on the market are made of wood and they are made in a number of styles. The boxes with a single entrance hole appeal to some of the birds, while the open fronted style seems to appeal to more of the pairs of breeding birds. Apparently this open front gives them the opportunity to arrange the entrance more to the pair's satisfaction. Even the soft-billed birds, such as the Shama Thrushes, will usually accept an open fronted wooden nest box, which will obviously need to be much larger than the types used for finches.

Birds will choose to use these wooden nestboxes in colder weather, probably because wood has far greater and better insulating qualities than any nestbox made of other materials, such as metal or plastic. The greatest disadvantage to these wooden nestboxes, regardless of their style, is the difficulty in cleaning them once the birds have used them for nesting. Also, the joints in these wooden boxes make ideal hiding places for the mites and lice that are always happy to make a home with the birds.

Enterprising manufacturers have tried to counter these nestbox disadvantages by making a nestbox out of plastic that you can easily disassemble for cleaning. The birds, if given a choice, will still choose the wooden boxes, perhaps because this is a known and natural material.

Another type of nesting receptacle that is commonly available on the market is the woven, wicker nesting container. These come in several sizes, and they are often acceptable to small birds that will not accept any of the standard wooden or plastic nesting receptacles. Especially when you fasten these in a thick bush or hide them in the clumps of grass that you have growing in your aviary, they will appeal readily to birds such as the waxbills.

For anyone who raises canaries, linnets, chaffinches, the siskins, or any of the serins, however, an open nesting receptacle is needed. Manufacturers have fabricated these for many years in both metal and plastic for the use of canary breeders. They come in at least three sizes to appeal to the various canary breeds. The small serins, such as the Green Singing Finch, *Serinus mozambicus*, and the Gray Singing Finch, *Serinus atrogularis*, will accept the smallest size of the metal canary nests.

Dealers are now offering the canary-style nests made from the woven wicker material that is also used for the enclosed finch nests. These neatly woven nesting receptacles appear very natural, and they will appeal not only to the canaries, but also to the other small avian species that use that style of nesting receptacle. The diamond Doves, *Geopelia cuneata*, are sure to accept them, and many of the small ground doves that breeders maintain will also accept them readily.

As many of the serins are such tiny birds, even the smallest canary nest is often too large for their comfort. In this case, there is a human commercial alternative that will do very nicely. It is called a tea strainer, and every Green Singing Finch that I have ever raised was raised by its parents in a tea strainer. You can easily attach a tea strainer securely in a hidden location, and the small serins will all be likely to accept this over any other commercial or natural nesting receptacle.

In addition to the nestboxes and nesting containers available commercially, you can make your own nesting receptacles. One of the commonest types is made with the use of a simple small coil of hardware cloth or one inch chicken wire that is about six inches in diameter. When you attach this small roll of wire in a protected location and make a rough nest in the coil with a mixture of nesting material, such as dried grass, shredded burlap or coconut fiber, many species of small birds will accept this as a nesting area. Many of the books on breeding birds and aviculture recommend this type of nesting receptacle.

Besides the small coil, you can use a larger roll of wire that is about three feet long and about two feet in diameter, stuff it rather tightly with hay, and then pull out some hay in several areas that will leave a hole that you can fashion into a rough nest. Any birds that accept this as a nesting site will further refine the opening and they will build their nest in this roll of hay very happily.

For many years, I have made two types of nesting receptacles for the birds that I have kept, and have never yet seen either of them used by any other breeder. For the finches, a size 2½ can serves the purpose very well. This is the wide, squatty looking can often used for tomatoes, peaches and pears. The trick is to use your can opener to open the can only half way -- in other words 180° instead of the full 360° or so cut that you normally use to open a metal can. Then, take a heavy spoon to pry and bend that open half of the lid up to a 90° angle from the remaining part of the attached lid.

When you attach this can in a cage or aviary, it makes an ideal nesting site for the birds with a ready made lip as an entrance perch. Though everyone asks me the question, "Don't the birds cut their feet on that sharp metal?", the answer is "No." I have raised thousands of Zebra Finches, *Taeniopygia guttata*, plus hundreds of finches of other varieties in these cans over the years, and have never yet had a bird cut its foot on one of these cans. The only disadvantage to these cans is that they are not the warmest possible nest for the birds during cold weather. The metal conducts the heat away from the nest too rapidly. Refer to Diagram 1 on the next page to illustrate exactly what one of these nesting cans looks like.

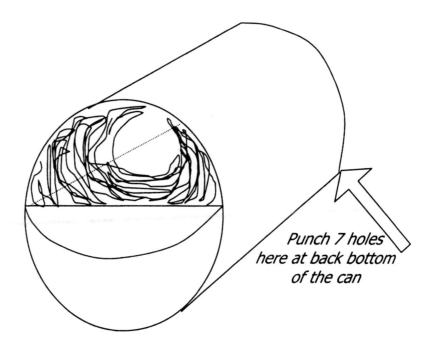

Diagram 1 - Number 2 ½ Can as a Nesting Site

When you use this specially opened can as a nesting site in a flight cage, you do not even need to fasten the can to the cage to make it stable. Simply brace the can with the end of the cage, and set the perch so that it is tight under the 90° lip. This locks the can in place between the perch and the end of the cage. You can easily lift it out at any time to check on eggs or babies. For this type of nesting can, I would also recommend that you punch about seven holes in the back bottom of the can, This will allow air circulation and will also serve as drainage holes if the nest should get wet in a driving rainstorm.

In addition to the nesting can drawn above, I have also often used a specially cut, folded and nailed piece of hardware cloth as a nesting site for the small doves. I have raised hundreds of Diamond Doves in nesting receptacles of this type, as well as dozens of the Cape Doves, *Oena capensis*, and Ruddy Ground Doves, *Columbina talpacoti*. The requirements for this type of nesting site are the simplest -- one piece of quarter-inch mesh hardware cloth cut to six inches wide and 7½ inches long. Make a 1½ inch cut in the center of the longer dimension of this piece of hardware cloth. See the illustration as Diagram 2 on the next page of the hardware cloth at this point.

Fold the two 1½ inch flanges up at a 90° angle from the main 6 by 6 inch surface of the piece of hardware cloth. Then fold the hardware cloth at about a 60° angle in the center along the line where you have made the cut, as illustrated on the next page in Diagram 3. This gives you a nicely cupped nesting receptacle. You can nail this to any reasonably flat surface with two short, galvanized roofing nails to form a perfect nesting site for the small doves. Be sure to put two nails into the overlapping flanges. If you use only one nail, the nesting receptacle can come loose and rotate, spilling the eggs or babies. With two nails, the nesting site always will be secure. The resulting nesting site is a somewhat concave nesting platform that is six inches square, and all of the small doves accept this as a nesting location very readily.

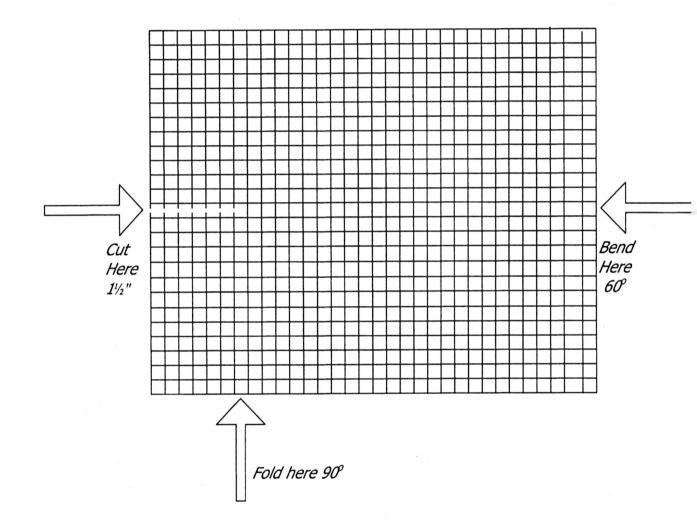

Cut
Here
1½"

Bend
Here
60°

Fold here 90°

Diagram 2 - Hardware Cloth for Dove Nest Showing Cut

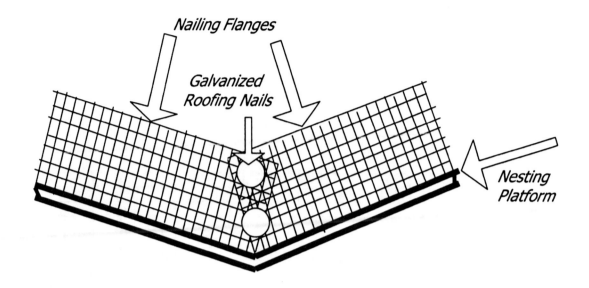

Diagram 3 - Nailing Flanges of the Nesting Platform

Perhaps the most successful nesting sites in any outdoor aviary are found in the clumps of grass that you have planted in the aviary. Refer to Chapter 11 for a more detailed coverage of the grasses available and how to use them most effectively. The birds will build their nests and hide them in the drooping blades of grass, and the nests will be very difficult to see or locate. Often you will not know that the birds are nesting until you flush one off of the nest in the grass while working in the aviary. These grass clumps give the birds a welcome feeling of safety and security, and there is no substitute for clumps of grass in an outdoor aviary. Unless you are raising such birds as budgerigars or canaries that will eat and destroy any plant in the aviary, by all means include the drooping grasses in any aviary of birds that you keep.

The most successful location for nesting sites that I have used in my aviaries for the small birds, including the small doves, consists of a treated fence post placed upright in their outdoor aviary. Plant a vine to grow up around the pole so that it will partly hide the nesting sites. Train the vines to grow up around the nesting sites, and you will have a perfect nesting arrangement for any of the small finches and doves. Honeysuckle vines are ideal for this use in many climate areas. When placed away from the outer walls of your aviary, this type of nesting arrangement will prevent predators outside the aviary from frightening the birds off of the nest at night.

You can also place cross members on this post, attaching them so that they go off in several directions. These cross pieces will provide an additional variety of good nesting sites for the birds in the aviary. As you train the vines to cover these cross pieces also, you can place nesting sites on the cross pieces for the birds. This is the most successful method of providing safe nesting sites for the birds that I have found.

Chapter 11

Plants and Landscaping
in the Aviary

Plants placed in an aviary create a number of advantages that will not be found in unplanted aviaries. First, and probably most important for the welfare of the birds, they provide hiding and nesting sites for all of the birds in the aviary. Many aviary birds prefer bushes or small, thick trees for their nest building, and these will also make excellent sites for placing artificial nesting receptacles. Vines and grasses will be ideal nesting sites for some species, and even hanging baskets of flowers can provide an excellent nesting location. Don't neglect the recycling effect that plants have, either; they absorb and use the nutrients dissolved from the bird droppings, while providing edible leaves and shoots for the birds to nibble on, ready-made and springy perches, and nesting and hiding spots for each species in the aviary. Each of these planting uses and possibilities will be discussed in detail in this chapter.

Perhaps the commonest mistake that aviculturists make in planting their aviaries is through planting too many plants for the size of the aviary. An aviary that is 16 feet by 16 feet, for example, has enough room for one small tree; two small bushes, no more that two feet in diameter; several clumps of small grasses; and perhaps a couple of hanging baskets. Though the grasses may be touching, the other plants need open space around them. This will provide the aviary birds with hiding and nesting areas, while still allowing open ground for birds like the doves, quails and waxbills that need these open areas for their exercise, courtship displays, and natural foraging activities.

Experience has shown that plants should never be allowed to grow within one foot of the outer aviary wire. This keeps the wire safe from stretching and tearing during severe winds from the growing plants pushing against it, and it also allows the birds a free flyway around the perimeter of the aviary. Most important, however, when the birds roost at night, they will not be near the outer wire of the aviary. Any climbing, nighttime visitor in the form of a cat, raccoon, opossum, or other natural predator, will not be able to get close to the birds, even if it climbs up the wire on the side of the aviary. This type of planting design goes a long ways toward preventing night panics among the birds. Night panics are sure to result in more injuries, death and abandoned nests than any other single factor in an outdoor aviary.

Other factors of design are also important when placing growing plants in any outdoor aviary. For best viewing of the birds, the open areas and the small plants should be in the front two-thirds of the aviary, while any taller plants should be in the rear. A small pond or running water should also be placed near the front of the aviary. In an aviary that is wider than it is deep, for example, a ten foot deep aviary with twenty feet across the front, a C-shaped planting is most attractive and effective. Plants should curve from the left front of the aviary around to the back and then curve up the right side of the aviary to the right front with open area to the front of the aviary within the 'C'. This provides the maximum of viewing area, while still allowing enough areas for the birds to feel secure and hidden when perching, resting and nesting. A planting in this design will provide secure nesting areas for a variety of birds in the aviary.

Though a tree will make the aviary a more natural place for the birds, many varieties of trees are not suitable for a small aviary. In any aviary that is less that 20 feet by 20 feet, use a tree that has small leaves. Small leaves or needles mean more branches for perching and hiding, and trees with smaller leaves are more easily trimmed and kept within the ideal size for the aviary location. Live oaks, laurel oaks, apple, wild cherry, spruce, fir, and short-needled pines are all ideal, and completely safe for the birds. In the more tropical locations and climate areas, I have seen podocarpus, bottlebrush, acacia and pomegranate used to good advantage. All of these can easily be kept trimmed to fit within the aviary, and they will provide a variety of hiding places and nesting sites for all of the birds in the aviary.

Don't neglect the small-leafed trees and bushes that are native in your local area, either. Often, even though they may not be available in a nursery, the local trees with small leaves are easily available, and they are ideal for use in a planted aviary, as well as being free. Many land owners are only too happy to have you dig up a few of their pest trees and shrubs, as long as you are neat with the job and fill in the resulting holes after you're finished. Since these are native to your own area, with adequate care they are certain to be hardy and healthy in your aviary, and they will make an excellent addition to any aviary environment.

Also, when you transplant from a natural location into your aviary, use a few of the common tricks that nurserymen frequently use when you do the transplanting., For example, it is best to root prune one side of the plant a month or so before moving the plant. Simply cut the roots halfway around the tree or shrub, and fill the dirt back. This will stimulate the growth of new feeder roots close to the plant. When you dig the plant up to transplant, dig a ball of root area about two inches wider than the half circle of your previous cutting of the roots. This will give the plant a much better chance of surviving the shock when you also cut the roots on the other side of the plant and lift it out for the transplanting. It is also a good idea to cut the limbs back to reduce the area that the roots must feed and supply with water.

Once you have cut back and transplanted the new plant into your aviary, take the time to sprinkle the leaves a couple of times a day, particularly on hot, sunny days. This will replace some of the water that the leaves lose that the roots cannot easily resupply until they have grown out into the soil of the aviary. Actually, this is good advice whenever you plant new shrubbery or trees anywhere, particularly when you have purchased those plants with bare roots. On rainy days, of course, nature will take of this for you.

A variety of bushes are also available for planting in an aviary. The dense boxwoods, barberries and small-leafed hollies are available in most nurseries, and they provide a dense cover and many potential nesting areas for the smaller birds. Each area of North America has its own landscaping specialties, and most of the small leafed shrubs are perfectly safe for the birds. Most local bird clubs will also maintain a listing of the known poisonous plants that do well in your local area to forewarn you about the danger of their use in the aviary. Junipers are available in any number of styles and growth habits in virtually every climate zone in North America, and all of the dozens of varieties of junipers are perfectly safe for the birds. The exotic hollies with dense growth habits and very small leaves are also all ideal for aviary planting. For birds, such as the waxbills, that feel most at home in thorny bushes, there are varieties of barberry available as landscape plants that are also ideal subjects for aviary planting.

The hollies, boxwoods and junipers are evergreen, and they will keep their leaves or needles throughout the year. The barberries are deciduous, and will lose their leaves in the winter. Again, don't neglect your local native shrubs, both the deciduous and evergreen types, as many of these will be ideal for use in your planted aviary, and they will be perfectly hardy and healthy in your aviary.

Two of my own favorites for aviary use in cold winter areas, where below freezing weather and snows are expected through every winter, are the Dwarf Mugho Pine, *Pinus mugo mughus*, and the Dwarf Alberta Spruce, *Picea glauca conica*. Both of these are very dense and slow growing, and they will need only minor trimming to keep them under control in the aviary planting. Further, both of these species are evergreen, so they will be available for the birds all through the year. These two plants will offer a choice of hidden nesting sites for all of the birds in the aviary and will provide a secure area for hiding and foraging, but they must be planted in full sun. For those birds that you keep outdoors for the winter, these two plants will provide an ideal roosting area that is sheltered from the worst of the wind and weather.

Vines with small leaves are quite useful in an aviary, as most varieties grow very fast, and they provide a dense hiding and nesting area for the birds. Honeysuckle has always been my favorite for aviary planting, as it is very fast growing, flowers freely attracting many insects for the birds, and as an added bonus, the flowers have a truly marvelous odor. In addition, honeysuckle is completely hardy through fairly cold, snowy winters. Should there be space in your aviary for only one plant, I would recommend that you choose honeysuckle. Though the fast growth of this vine will require frequent trimming and control, there is no better all around plant more suitable for an outdoor aviary. Also, for other options, check with your local nurseries for other vines that are hardy and popular in your own area.

As discussed in Chapters 1 and 10, the most successful nesting location I have used for birds in the outdoor aviary, including doves, waxbills and other small finches, consisted of a simple treated fence post placed upright in their aviary. Plant a honeysuckle vine or another safe and fast growing vine to grow up around the pole so that it will partly hide the nesting sites. Train the vines to grow up around the nesting sites, and you will have a perfect nesting arrangement for any of the small doves, finches, and softbills. Honeysuckle vines are ideal for this use in many climate areas. As an added bonus, when placed away from the outer walls of the aviary, this setup will prevent the finches from being frightened off of the nest at night by predators outside the aviary. In effect, this creates a dense, artificial tree anywhere in the aviary that you need one, and it is a most effective method of providing safe and useful perching, hiding and nesting areas for the birds in the aviary.

The treated fenceposts are very solid, reasonably cheap, and extremely long-lasting. I have dug them up after 9 years, and the wood is still perfectly firm with no rot nor decomposition evident. They should last in the aviary for at least 20 years, and probably much longer. Unless you're raising woodpeckers, creepers or nuthatches that naturally climb on the wood rather than perching, the chemical treatment in the wood will present no danger at all to the health of the birds. For birds of those species you should use a natural, untreated wooden post that still has the bark attached.

When using the chemically treated posts, after only a few weeks, the surface chemicals used in the wood treatment will be counteracted by the action of wind and sunlight, and the post will assume a weathered, natural look. This aging will increase your safety margin, though I have encountered no problems even when using the freshly treated posts in the aviary. Even after aging, the chemical treatment is still active within the wood, however, and decomposition of this treated post will progress only very slowly.

As a further tip on this method of establishing a nesting security area in your aviary, check out your local farm stores and suppliers of these pressure treated fence posts. The treatment process causes some posts to warp badly. Though one of these crooked posts makes an unsightly fence when used for this purpose, it is still perfect for an outdoor aviary. Further, a dealer is often very happy to let you have that badly crooked post for a very substantial discount. Merchandise thus 'damaged' is very difficult for any dealer to sell, and they are usually glad to get rid of these crooked posts. Certainly, the birds in your aviary will have no objection to a warped fence post, and once the vine that you plant grows around the post completely, you won't be able to see the fence post at all.

This use of damaged merchandise is a way to make a substantial saving on the cost of your aviary and other areas around the home. When using 2 inch by 4 inch mesh rolls of wire for deer and animal protection around my young trees, I noted that one of the rolls of wire at the farm store had been run over by a truck. The bad dent in the roll of wire did not in any way damage it as a tree protector, so I asked the manager if he would give me a discount on that damaged roll of wire. The manager was very happy to get rid of the damaged roll, and gave me a 50% discount on the price. Don't ever be hesitant to ask if there is a piece of damaged merchandise that you can use. You can save a substantial amount on the cost of your aviary and bird keeping efforts this way.

For many of the doves, quails and finches, the best possible plants to provide a feeling of security for the birds, food in the form of the ripening seed-heads, and hidden locations for nesting and breeding, are the long, drooping grasses. There are a huge variety of these that can be used, native to every continent except Antarctica, but the most readily available in nurseries in mild climates are several varieties of fountain grass. For climates without freezing winter temperatures, you can use the red fountain grass and the white fountain grass, these names used because of the color found in their leaves and ripening seedheads. These two types of grass have different growth habits, also, and the use of both types is best to provide a variety of hidden locations.

Most varieties of fountain grass are not hardy and will die out in any winter area where temperatures go below freezing. However, one hardy type, *Pennisetum alopecuroides*, is used widely in horticulture. One of the varieties of this Fountain Grass has attractive, reddish seed heads, and another has black seed heads. Use this variety of fountain grass in any area with cold winters and frequent snowfalls.

In areas of colder winters, there are a number of other varieties of beautiful grasses that are used widely in landscaping and are eminently adaptable for use in a planted aviary. At least two commercial varieties of *Miscanthus sinensis* are used in landscaping. These are known by the common names of Maiden Grass and Flame Grass. Both adapt well to aviary usage.

Other species of grasses offer an endless variety of growth habit, leaf color, and seedhead coloring. As examples, there are varieties of Sedge Grass that will do very well in aviaries. The Copperleaf Sedge, *Carex flagillifera*, in particular, has a brownish foliage that looks much like dead grass and will attract grass-loving birds in any aviary. With a smaller grass, such as the *Festuca* varieties, in a mixed planting with Sedge Grass, you will have developed an area that is perfectly natural for any of the waxbills. Should you be specializing in the mannikins, you will find that Reed Grass, *Calamagrostis acutiflora*, is a tall, hardy, perennial grass that mannikins love for perching and foraging.

For many of the waxbills, in particular, there is no nesting site that they will accept over a clump of drooping grasses. The birds build their covered nests and carefully camouflage them within the grass clumps. You may not even realize that the birds are nesting until you flush the hen off of her nest in the grass as you do your daily aviary chores.

If your aviary is large, you can also use Pampas Grass. This grass has huge, white seedheads that can reach a height of ten feet or more under ideal conditions. An additional horticultural variety of Pampas Grass is available that has pink seedheads. The blades of grass in a Pampas Grass clump are stiff, sharp, and finely serrated. They are dangerous to anyone who brushes against them, and they will cut exposed flesh deeply if you should push by one of the Pampas Grass clumps without thinking.

The cowboys of Argentina don't wear those heavy, leather leg protections for fun, either. Pampas grass can be dangerous stuff, and riding through it without heavy protection is unwise in the extreme. Also, as pampas grass becomes so large, it can be a perfect hiding place for rats and mice if they should somehow gain access to the aviary. Aviary security from rats and the other predators is discussed in detail in Chapter 5. Nevertheless, the finches absolutely love the clumps of pampas grass, and I once had four different species of waxbills nesting simultaneously in the same clump of pampas grass.

A visit to your local nurseries will enable you to see which of the grasses will do best in your area. There are literally hundreds of varieties that are available either through local nurseries or through the extensive variety of mail order catalogs that are available from many of the large nurseries that specialize in shipping. If you can try several varieties of ornamental grass in your aviary, you will soon know which will do the best under your local conditions.

For the ground of the outdoor aviary, you can design and make several different arrangements. One of my favorites is a light mulching with small pine needles or spruce needles. These needles are usually available in abundance under any of the spruces, firs or large pines with short needles. A half inch layer of these on any spot of bare ground makes a marvelous mulch, and the covering is light enough that the birds can easily move it around to get at the seeds and other bits of food that filter through the mulch. Some of the seeds will always be missed, however, and these will grow and provide valuable green food for the birds in the aviary. A thin layer of small bark chips will also accomplish the same function.

There are several noteworthy advantages to light mulching of this type. First, light mulching helps to keep the soil damp, especially during hot weather. In soils with a high clay content, this is especially valuable, as clay soils will become as hard as bricks when they completely dry out. Another advantage to the light covering of mulch on the ground is that mulch serves to hold the soil in place during heavy rains and wind. Particularly if your aviary is on a slope, water running on bare soil is sure to wash away large amounts of the soil and can easily cause a gully to form. This soil loss is decidedly unattractive in a planted aviary, and running water carving away the soil in your aviary shows a total lack of understanding of the natural balance of nature on the part of the aviculturist.

Even grass clippings scattered on the soil of the aviary will serve to keep the soil protected temporarily. At one location, I used nothing but grass clippings to mulch the flower beds, and the resulting flowers were spectacular. The only real disadvantage to the use of grass clippings is that they decompose so rapidly. Through the action of worms and bacteria, grass clippings used as a mulch will be completely decomposed and mixed in the soil within about a month, while pine or spruce needles may last for years. Of course, this decomposition adds a huge amount of organic matter and mineral nutrients to the soil, and any plants in the soil with roots in that area will get the full benefit of the extra nutrients.

In damp areas that are mostly shady, a few low-growing ferns will provide an interesting contrast in the plants for the aviary. Every area has its own variety of native ferns that will be perfectly safe and at home in your own climate zone. Commercially grown ferns may be native to other, warmer areas and may not be nearly so hardy in your climate zone. Nevertheless, many ferns are available for areas where winter freezes are common, and if you live in a more tropical location, there is a huge variety of possible ferns from a variety of families and genera that can be of effective use in the planting and landscaping of an aviary with shady spots.

A planted aviary always offers a small area where seeds can sprout and grow. Many of the birds in the aviary will eat the tender shoots from the sprouting seeds. The plants in the cabbage family make particularly tender and succulent green food for any of the birds that may want it. Kale and rapeseed are two of the best for this purpose. The serins in particular love these small tender leaves, and when keeping these birds, you should always offer small leaves of this type on a daily basis. Any of the cereal grains will form tender green shoots, and I have even seen doves walking along snipping and eating the tops of the sprouting grasses.

All birds will accept living green food if it is presented in a way that is acceptable to them. Most of the softbilled birds cannot bite chunks out of a leaf as canaries and serins do, but they will break off and eat the tender shoots of sprouting grasses. I have also observed doves methodically picking the buds off of a planting of impatiens. Though they would not touch the stems, leaves, or flowers, those little flower buds were exactly what they wanted, and they picked and ate them in huge quantities.

After the initial planting and fertilizing of your landscaped aviary, it will never again be necessary to fertilize any of the plants. There is no better fertilizer than bird droppings, and in a naturally planted aviary, the droppings will decompose rapidly on the ground of the aviary. Rains will wash the droppings off of the leaves and needles of the trees and shrubs, and the water will carry the nutrients in these droppings into the soil, where the soil microorganisms will break them down into their constituent elements. Once this breakdown occurs, the roots of the plants will absorb and utilize these nutrients.

The soil's bacteria, other microorganisms, and earthworms will certainly appreciate this bountiful supply of high-nutrient droppings, also. In any area that stays permanently damp, you will see small, round translucent or transparent balls appearing. This is the sign of a really good soil, for these are the egg casings of earthworms. Each of these will hatch into one or more tiny earthworms, and if you are raising softbills that will need a steady supply of earthworms for feeding their young, this is one of the cheapest and best ways of providing earthworms for their consumption as a nestling food for the babies.

A few years of this constant recycling and the addition of organic matter will add several inches to the level of the soil in the aviary. Before things get out of hand, you will have to shovel out some of this extra, composted soil, or your grasses and short plants eventually will be buried. Also, many kinds of trees can and will be killed if the soil builds up around their trunks.

This is a good place to mention that the commonest cause of death in trees that you plant is because the soil was allowed to build up around the trunk of the newly planted tree. Nurseries often have trees that have been planted too deeply in the pots, and if you plant them in the ground at the same depth, they will sit there looking bad for several years, and then they will die. The only trees that I have seen tolerate this treatment with no damage are the willows, elders, and alders. Most other trees will be killed if soil is allowed to build up around their trunks.

When you plant a tree, make sure that the trunk is above ground so that you can see where the roots begin to grow out from the trunk. As long as the base of those roots is showing above the soil level, the tree is not too deep. If you feel that this leaves the tree too unstable in the soil, place a large, heavy rock on each side of the trunk, close, but not shading the trunk. These rocks will hold the base of the tree steady in any wind or rain, and they are far more effective than staking until the tree can get its roots well established in the new location. I never stake any tree that I plant, as through the years, I have found that unstaked trees form far sturdier and straighter trunks as they grow.

There are always places to use all of the rich extra soil that has formed in your aviary from the constant decomposition of the food and droppings, and the action of the bacteria and the earthworms. Topdressing the thin, anemic areas of your lawn is one possibility. Thin grass or bare spots in the lawn means that the nutrients in the soil are used up or perhaps are unavailable to the grass, either from excess alkalinity or excess acidity. Adding this rich, highly organic soil from the aviary will replace any of the nutrients that are missing from the soil where the grass is growing poorly. There is no soil so infertile nor so barren that it cannot be greatly helped by the addition of the composted soil from the aviaries.

A second use for this extra aviary soil is to add the soil to your flower beds. The flowering plants will certainly appreciate the new soil, and they will bloom much more profusely. The flowers will also be larger and the colors will be richer and more vibrant. An extension of this idea is to use the extra soil from the aviary as potting soil for your house plants. Based on my own experience, this will result in the most lush and beautiful house plants that you have ever seen!

I once performed an experiment with several peach trees that I purchased early one spring at a local nursery. They were normal, dormant, bare root trees, with trunks about one-half inch in diameter. After planting them in the back yard, I immediately began spreading the cleanings from my finch cages around the trees. The trees became established in record time, and they grew very rapidly. The larger the trees grew, the wider the finch manure was spread, and the more I put around each tree. The result of this experiment was nothing short of astounding. In the second year, I harvested a small group of peaches, just enough to appreciate the differences and flavors in each variety that I had planted. By the end of the third year, these peach trees were about twelve feet tall and wide, with trunks a full six inches in diameter. And also in their third year of growth, with the abundant supply of nutrients in the finch manure, each of those trees bore over three *bushels* of beautiful and delicious peaches.

The rich soils that are created in this natural process will also cause the plants in the aviary to grow and expand rapidly in a similar manner. Those of you who are accustomed to birds that grow to a maximum size and stay at that size for the rest of their lives often forget that the plants in an aviary are in a completely different living kingdom. Plants are virtually never at their maximum size. Plants of all kinds will continue to grow as long as they live. Without your constant attention, a small, attractive planting in a very short time will become an impenetrable jungle. Though some plants, such as the cacti and succulents, grow very slowly, most other varieties will grow several feet in the course of a year. Some vines under ideal conditions may grow as much as 15 or 20 feet each year. Though a few of the species that we keep will love this jungle environment, most of them will not. The majority of our aviary inhabitants come from areas of grassland or savanna with only scattered clumps of trees or bushes.

Some aviculturists prefer a concrete floor for their aviaries. As mentioned elsewhere, I tried this at one time and found concrete as an aviary floor to be very unsatisfactory. It turned out to be a high maintenance floor that never looked good, and when the concrete became wet from a rain, it became dangerously slippery. All of the beneficial effects of living growth and decomposition that are found in a dirt floor are not found in a concrete floor, unless you add plants in containers to the aviary. After trying this concrete floor, there was nothing I could point to as an advantage of having the concrete floor instead of the base of natural earth for the aviary.

When you trim the plants in the aviary, don't shear them. The plants in an aviary should appear natural, and shearing gives the impression of a formal garden, as well as eliminating the varying length of limbs and branches that the birds need for perching. Trim one branch back at a time with a pair of hand trimmers that you prefer to use. A variety of types are manufactured, and you can choose the one that you like the best. This selective trimming will still keep the aviary plants looking natural and serving their primary purpose as perching, hiding and nesting places for the birds in the aviary.

Don't ever be afraid to trim your aviary plants to keep them at the size you want. This will not harm the plants in the least, but failure to do this will result in an aviary so dense that you will not even be able to see the birds within, and you certainly won't be able to catch them successfully when necessary. Also, never allow plants, trees or vines to grow through the wire of the aviary. These living, growing things will exert a tremendous amount of pressure, and a tree limb growing through the wire of the aviary will in time exert enough pressure to tear the wire from its supports, creating a space large enough to allow the birds to escape or to allow snakes and other predators to gain access to the aviary.

Allowing the plants to create a jungle will negate several of the primary requirements for a successful aviary. The fact that the capture of the birds will become impossible has already been mentioned. Also, viewing the birds will become very difficult, as they will always be hidden in the foliage. Any of the birds that come from grassy, open areas will be unlikely to breed in an area that is too thick, as they simply will not feel secure without several feet of open space around them at all times. The ground area will become so shady that grasses will not grow there, and any of the birds that need grass clumps for nesting and security will not breed under these conditions. Finally, a constantly shady area grows all types of molds and fungi, as these conditions are perfect for these primitive plants.

You want to keep any molds and fungi far away from your birds. These are plants that exist mainly as parasites and saprophytes without chlorophyll, and they produce as by-products of their life cycles the strongest and most dangerous poisons known. These poisons go by the technical names 'mycotoxins' and 'aflatoxins'. Even microscopic amounts of these poisons can be deadly to us as well as to the birds. Merely touching the poisonous white mushroom, *Amanita phalloides*, leaves enough poison on your finger to kill you, if you should eat it with some food without washing your hands first. A number of the mushrooms in the genus *Amanita* are poisonous.

The poisonous by-products of molds growing on damp, sprouting seeds are enough to kill any bird that eats that seed. Most deaths of aviary birds from poisoning can be traced to improper handling and feeding of damp items, such as sprouting seeds. Fortunately, these microorganisms will not grow in the sunlight, so any seeds sprouted in sunlight should be completely safe for the birds. Frequent washing in chlorinated water is also effective in preventing the growth of dangerous molds. Two old standard veterinary disinfectants, Nolvasan® and Virosan®, as well as newer ones now in use, diluted in water and used to wash sprouted seeds and other damp feeds, are also very effective in controlling molds, fungal spores, and viruses. One of the newer veterinary disinfectants that have been tested by aviculturists and seem to be safe for the birds, their cages and aviaries is PARVO-LAN-128, available from Glo-marr Products, Inc., Lawrencebury, Kentucky 40342, telephone 800-228-7387. This product is especially effective against viruses. Another very effective new product is Kennel Sol, manufactured by Alpha Tech Pet, Inc., Lexington, Massachusetts 02173.

Lest you begin to feel that disinfecting will kill all microorganisms and make anything perfectly safe permanently, you should know that all of the spores, bacteria, viruses and other germs are constantly floating in the air. And not just here and there, but everywhere in unimaginable numbers. Actual counts of the number of living things floating in a cubic foot of so-called clean air are mind-boggling. In addition to all of the smog, smoke, gas fumes and other trace materials in the air, each cubic foot of clean air contains *between 40,000 and 60,000 living things*. A cubic foot of air is only 12 inches by 12 inches by 12 inches, yet every cubic foot of air contains enough life to repopulate an area of sterilized soil within a matter of minutes.

Fortunately, our bodies and the birds' bodies are able to breathe the air with all of this life in it, filter the living things out of the air, neutralize them, and remain in perfect health. Only when malnutrition destroys the protective mucous membranes in the breathing passages do these living things in the air we breathe start to grow and reproduce, causing colds, flu, and a host of other ills that most people consider 'normal'. Diseases are not normal, and any healthy body can throw off even injected cancer cells without any danger of contracting the disease. For a complete coverage of the subject of avian health and nutrition, refer to my full length books, *Nutrition of Finches and Other Cage Birds*, published in 1981, and *Avian Nutrition*, published in 1999, with a second edition published in 2003.

Chapter 12

Open and Sheltered Areas

As an initial statement on the subject of this chapter, you should be aware that the open areas of the aviary are the most important. After all, the outdoors is always open, and it is the natural habitat of all birds. This chapter will cover the construction of the covered and enclosed areas in an outdoor aviary, and also will discuss how they can be made to be of the most positive benefit to the birds in the aviary.

Exposure to sunlight and fresh air are important factors in keeping our aviary birds in perfect health. Sunlight and air circulation are very effective disinfectants, as most microorganisms cannot live and grow in the presence of sunlight. This is particularly true of the molds, fungi and harmful microorganisms that complete their life cycles in the dampness of deep shade.

As I stressed in Chapter 1, the open area of an outdoor aviary should be in an area of full sunlight. Locating an aviary in the shade is asking for trouble. Any shady location will dry out far more slowly after a rain than will a sunny area. The longer this shady area stays damp, the more likely it is that the ground and the framing surfaces of the aviary will begin to show signs of molds and fungi. These visible shade-loving saprophytes are certainly bad enough, but the microorganisms that also begin growing in the shade cause the worst problems that you are likely to experience in any outdoor aviary. As by-products of their normal life cycles, these shade-loving microorganisms produce the most potent poisons and toxins known. These dangerous poisons go by the technical names 'aflatoxins' and 'mycotoxins'. They are among the most toxic and deadly substances known to science, and if ingested, they will kill humans as quickly as they will kill any of the birds that have eaten food that was contaminated with these toxins.

Don't forget that most of the plants that are suitable for an outdoor aviary also require full sunlight for their best growth, normal development and for their health. Any aviary plant that requires sunlight will do very poorly in a shaded portion of the aviary. This is especially true of all of the conifers that were mentioned in Chapter 11, and is also true of most of the deciduous trees. If you don't know whether a plant requires sunlight or if it will do acceptably in the shade, ask someone who knows. This information is also widely available in the wealth of written material on plants and landscaping that are always available at any library or bookstore. Also, any plant that is under the sheltered portion of the aviary will not get water from the natural rains that soak the open part of the aviary, and you will have to water any plants in the covered area by hand. In exceptionally dry climates and in dry periods at any time of the year, you will need to supply water for these growing plants in the aviary, just as you would for the landscaping around your house and garden.

Planning for an outdoor aviary requires a knowledge of the climatic conditions that the birds will face in your area and how much protection from the weather they will need. In the wild, of course, birds always manage to find areas to shelter when it rains. Also, the feathers of most birds repel water to a certain extent. In the ducks, geese, swans and other water birds, of course, this feather waterproofing has reached its highest development. Most of the birds that we keep in our aviaries, however, will need some shelter available on rainy days. Sheltered nesting sites for the birds are especially important if we are to maximize the production of young ones in the aviary. A nest that becomes soaking wet or a nest that is built in a nesting receptacle that holds water usually will cause the parent birds to abandon the nest.

In the colder climates where you can expect freezing weather and snow daily through the winter months, a covered area is a necessity. In most of the cold climates, an enclosed area is also advisable, unless the birds you are raising all are of the species that sleep in a cozy nest. However, any of the birds that are roosting on perches in temperatures that go far below freezing are in danger of freezing their toes and their feet.

As an interesting note on cold weather, I spent over three years near Fairbanks, Alaska. Most of the non-migratory birds in that northern area have feathers on their feet to keep their feet warm through the bitterly cold and dark months of winter. However, I was amazed to see ravens with feathers fluffed to keep warm, but with bare feet stomping around in the snow hunting food and tidbits at temperatures of 40 below zero (this temperature is the same on both the Fahrenheit and the Centigrade thermometers) and even colder. It was intriguing in the extreme to watch this and to wonder why these ravens were not freezing their feet at temperatures this bitterly cold. Many years passed before I was able to discover the true answer to this puzzle. The ravens have a natural glycerin antifreeze in their feet. This glycerin keeps their feet from freezing and keeps the blood liquid and circulating even at temperatures of 50° below zero, Fahrenheit, and colder.

In a mild climate, the purpose of a covered area in the outdoor aviary is to allow the aviary birds a protected spot when it rains. For most mild climates, simply covering half of the top of the aviary with a clear or opaque covering will be sufficient to protect the birds adequately from rain. However, any minimal covering of this type will not protect the birds from climbing predators. Using a covering material for an aviary does not necessarily mean that the area below the covering will be dark and damp. This will only happen if you cover the aviary with a solid, dark type of material, such as plywood, boards or shingles. The opaque sheets of polycarbonate and fiberglass let most of the light through, and if the aviary already provides some shaded areas for the birds, you can use the completely clear sheets of these materials to let all of the sunlight through so that even the covered area receives full sunlight.

Framing and building your aviary, the security measures necessary, and the organization of the interior of the aviary have been covered in other chapters. When you begin planning the covered areas, there are additional factors to consider. In other chapters I have advised you to put hardware cloth over the framing even in areas that are to be covered, since strong winds can tear the sheeting off of the covered areas and will allow the birds to escape if hardware cloth is not placed under those protective sheets. Nothing short of a major carnivorous predator, a tornado, a runaway vehicle, or a major hurricane will be able to exert enough force to tear the hardware cloth off of the framing.

As I stressed in Chapter 1, in those milder climate areas where simply covering the roof of half of the aviary is adequate to protect the birds, be certain to plan that portion of the aviary so that the roof of the aviary is sloped. A sloping roof will allow water to drain off easily. If the roof is flat, there is a very real possibility of heavy, drenching rains building up water on the roof to the point that it will leak through the covering material. A steep slope is not necessary, unless, of course, you live in an area that gets deep accumulations of snow. In any mild climate, a gentle slope of ½ inch per foot is usually adequate. This amounts to 4 inches of slope in an aviary roof that is 8 feet wide, and this will be adequate to allow constant drainage even in heavy rains. In central and south Florida, southern Texas and southern California, this type of simple roof covering is usually quite adequate to protect the birds from exposure to adverse weather conditions. Keep in mind however, that the simple roof covering does not provide any predator protection for the sides of the aviary.

The climatic conditions in other areas in the southern half of the 48 contiguous states vary widely from one region to the next, and also from one year to the next. While a simple aviary roof covering may be adequate in the southern, south central and southwestern states in some years, in other years these states may experience cold fronts that will be too severe for the birds in outdoor aviaries with only roof covering. This will require that you use some covering for the sides of at least part of the aviary. Using the polycarbonate or fiberglass sheeting halfway down the sides of the aviary for the covered area will provide protection from the weather, as well as protection from climbing predators. If your aviary is seven feet high, two sheets of the covering material placed horizontally will bring the protection down four feet from the top. If you place the material vertically, you will have to cut it to the proper length.

When you enclose the covered area in this manner on all four sides, the enclosed area will be warmer, both from the heat that the birds generate and from the light that passes through to warm the air. Special pieces of wood are made to close the ends of the sheeting so that it retains the warmer air better. Caulking between the pieces of wood and between the wood and the sheeting is also advisable in areas where sub-freezing temperatures are common. As I also noted in Chapter 1, be sure that the filler pieces that you use are purchased at the same place as the protective sheeting, as the different manufacturers of these materials use slightly different dimensions for the corrugations, and they are not interchangeable.

When covering an area of this type for the birds, be sure to allow a place for easy access to the enclosed area for yourself. This is necessary for maintenance, cleaning, nest-checking, and any other task requiring access to the enclosed area. In some milder climate areas, this can be simply a matter of scooting under the covering material. However, in colder areas, you may need an actual door for access to the covered portion of the aviary.

A more careful plan and a more comfortably enclosed and heated indoor area for the birds may be required for the covered area of an outdoor aviary that is built to withstand winter temperatures that remain well below freezing for weeks at a time. If the temperature extremes are severe, you may have to install a double layer of the clear aviary covering with several inches of dead air space between these covering layers for insulation. This dead air space will prevent the rapid loss of heat that occurs when the aviary covering is installed in a single layer only.

The covered area for this type of cold weather aviary should extend to the ground, of course, and even below the ground level for a few inches to provide the extra separation that may keep the soil within the covered portion of the aviary from freezing. A small entrance for the birds at ground level only needs to be a few inches tall and perhaps a foot wide. This will allow the birds access to the protected area once they become used to the location of the entrance area. It is best not to place new birds in an aviary of this type in the middle of winter, as they will not be familiar with the covered area, and may not be able to find the entrance to that area readily. With the new birds that you introduce during a warmer period, you will be giving them a number of days or weeks to become used to the covered area and its low entrance.

You can also raise the floor level under the covered area by six inches or a foot with a short ramp leading up from the ground level entrance for the birds. Having this entrance lower than the level of the covered area with an upward sloping entrance will also go a long ways toward keeping the warmer air within the covered area, while still giving the birds free access to both the open area of the aviary and the covered area.

Another trick that you must employ in a cold weather aviary is to place the highest perches within the covered area. Birds will naturally head for the highest perches in the aviary for the night, and if that highest set of perches is in the covered area of the aviary, they will always be under the covered area and warm for the night.

As a final note, having a pair of Button Quail, *Coturnix chinensis*, in any aviary of small birds is a major advantage. You will also see the scientific name for this species listed as *Excalfactoria chinensis* in many references. Young finches, softbills and doves often leave the nest early and nearly unable to fly. On cold nights babies on the floor of the aviary will not be able to keep warm and they will die. However, as the Button Quail huddle for warmth in a covered secure area, any fledgling that is still unable to fly well will crawl in underneath them. I've never seen a pair of Button Quail refuse this sanctuary to these fledgling babies of any species, and it is indeed a warm sight to see baby finches and doves both peering out from under the warm brooding of a pair of these quail. Through the years, having a pair of these Button Quail in every outdoor aviary has saved the lives of untold hundreds of my fledglings that were able to crawl in under them for brooding through the night.

Chapter 13

The Indoor Aviary

Building an aviary indoors will be a distinctly different experience from the construction of an outdoor aviary. The only real similarity is the need to keep the birds from escaping. Protection from weather is not necessary, as the house serves this function. Also, though protection from pets may be needed, no protection from wildlife will be necessary. As natural lighting conditions are not present indoors, this must be taken into consideration in addition in any of the plans for the design and construction of an indoor aviary.

The first requirement is a decision as to where the indoor aviary will be located. Kitchens and dining rooms are usually not the best location, as even the most perfectly designed indoor aviary will result in some dust and scattered feathers. Though all of this may not bother you in the least, virtually everyone has relatives or guests in the kitchen and dining room sooner or later. The dust, feathers and odors coming from an indoor aviary are decidedly unappetizing, and are likely to make some of your guests positively ill. An aviary placed in the kitchen or dining room is definitely not the best way to win friends and influence people.

A bathroom might be an ideal place to locate the indoor aviary, since most bathrooms are designed to be easily cleaned and vented. However, unless you live in a true mansion with huge bathrooms, the size of the bathroom alone usually will rule out this location for an aviary of any size. At any rate, keep this option in mind, as I have seen larger bathrooms that have a blank, unused wall that would be ideal for a small aviary for birds. As architects' designs for bathrooms rarely include large windows, lighting will certainly be more of a problem for a bathroom aviary than it would be in an airy atrium.

A wide hallway might be an ideal location for an indoor aviary. A long, narrow aviary, perhaps only one and one-half to two feet wide, would hold the smaller birds very effectively, but would need special arrangements for access. An aviary that is too small for you to enter for cleaning, feeding, and catching birds must be designed to enable you to reach every corner of it simultaneously from the access locations.

Some serious planning would have to go into the lighting, also, as hallways in any home are not normally designed with bright lighting in mind.

A large bedroom might be a good location for a small aviary that is well designed to minimize feather residue and dust. The control of dust in a bedroom location is crucial, as sleeping in a dusty area is certainly not a good idea. Our bodies struggle all day long to filter out all of the dust and microorganisms in the air we breathe, and sleeping in a dusty area will overwhelm your body's defenses and will likely result in constant coughing, breathing problems, sinus congestion and also an increased susceptibility to the diseases caused by airborne microorganisms.

One of the best places for an indoor enclosure for birds is an atrium. The atrium is designed as an area for plants and as an indoor garden, and will have enough windows or overhead windows and skylights to allow for the health and growth of a variety of plants. The traditional Roman atrium was an open area in the center of the home, but the climate in most North American locations is not suitable for an atrium in the traditional Roman style. Many people now apply the name 'atrium' to any area with overhead windows or skylights and spacious windows that will allow the growth of a variety of plants. An aviary will fit in perfectly in any area of this type. As an atrium is usually a fairly large area, you may be able to fit in several small aviaries for a variety of birds. Unfortunately, most modern homes do not have an atrium, and any area of this type will be far more common in the warmer climate areas.

In many southern U. S. homes and especially in Florida, often you will find a separate room called a sunroom or 'Florida Room', which is designed to admit a maximum amount of light and sunlight for rest and relaxation. This room is somewhat similar to an atrium, but usually it is under the main roof of the home with no overhead windows or skylights, having instead banks of windows on at least two sides to take advantage of the mild climate. This type of room can also be an ideal location for a small indoor aviary, since the banks of windows will provide the open and well lighted conditions that are the best for an aviary of birds.

Before you begin any construction of an indoor aviary, a great deal of planning and thought are necessary. Several of the types of construction materials suitable for a large, outdoor aviary are overkill when you are contemplating the construction of an indoor aviary. The indoor aviary will not be exposed to severe weather conditions, so there is no need for either pressure-treated lumber, stainless steel or even steel to resist the forces of nature.

Kiln-dried lumber is the most economical framing material for an indoor aviary, and it is also the easiest framing material to shape and handle. Since no wind nor weather conditions are necessary for the strength, the 2" x 2" lumber is usually quite adequate for the framing of an indoor aviary. Do keep in mind, however, that all of the 2 by 2 lumber is a little difficult to work with, and you will have to drill pilot holes for either the nails or the screws that you will be using to fasten the framing together. Still, as was covered in the chapter on aviary framing materials, the 2" by 4" lumber will be your best buy. For fastening the framing material, regular nails or screws will do the job nicely. Only in places that are likely to get wet from the birds' bathing and drinking is there a possible need for the use of stainless steel fasteners.

Aluminum framing is a second type of framing that is available in a variety of sizes, lengths, and angles that can be used in indoor aviaries. For indoor use, the angle aluminum or square aluminum pieces that you are most likely to be working with will give a polished and professional look to any indoor aviary. Though this material is far more expensive than wood, for an indoor application, you want your aviary to look as good as possible.

You can also use plastic framing in the form of PVC pipe or any of the other plastic materials that are available for water systems, carports or for protected outside storage areas. You can easily adapt these for use in framing your indoor aviary. Joint designs in a variety of angles and with a variety of outlets will be suitable for corners and joints for the framing of the indoor aviary.

As recommended for outside aviaries, I also recommend the use of the ¼ inch mesh hardware cloth as the wire covering for any indoor aviary. This smaller mesh wire will keep a lot of the aviary mess and feathers within the aviary, rather than allowing this material to sift through the wire to lay on the floor. Also birds and birdseed draw mice. The last thing you want in your house is mice that have been drawn there by the birds and the feed in the indoor aviary. The ¼ inch mesh hardware cloth will prevent any mouse that somehow gains access to the house from being able to enter the indoor aviary. Lest you think this completely unlikely, remember that your pet cats love to catch mice and carry them around, still alive and kicking. If the cat should bring the live mouse inside the house, the aviary would provide a welcome refuge for it when the cat became distracted and let the mouse go free.

The flooring for your indoor aviary should be of a material that is easily cleaned. The very best for the purpose of an indoor aviary is a type of flooring called terrazzo, which is found mainly in Florida. Commercial buildings sometimes use terrazzo flooring, since it is so easy to keep clean. A terrazzo floor is a floor that is poured from a mortar which is liberally and heavily laced with very small marble chips. Once the mortar is leveled, sets and dries, the contractor polishes the surface until the floor looks like a single piece of ceramic tile. Of course, this type of flooring requires a solid, stable and permanent concrete base, as any flexing or settling will cause cracks in the finished terrazzo flooring. Also, as the terrazzo forms a single surface with no joints or breaks, cleaning and maintaining this terrazzo flooring is remarkably easy.

Another of the better types of flooring for aviary use is ceramic tile. Ceramic floor tile is also easily cleaned and makes an attractive floor that is adaptable for a variety of purposes. Here again, for the best results, a completely solid and stable surface is required for the installation of ceramic tile. Any flexing or movement may cause cracks between the individual tiles and in the worst cases, you will have cracks in the ceramic tiles themselves.

Hardwood flooring is another possibility for the interior flooring material where you plan to build your indoor aviary. Though hardwood flooring is not as impervious to damage as are the terrazzo and tile floor coverings, hardwood flooring is the next best thing. A well sealed and finished hardwood floor will perform quite adequately as an aviary base for your indoor aviary, as long as you use nothing in the aviary that will scratch or cause damage to the floor.

The versatility of the terrazzo flooring and the tile flooring, as well as the hardwood flooring, are all the more important as flooring for your indoor aviary for another reason. Should you ever want to sell your house, or should you be forced to sell your house, the floor without the aviary over it will still be constructed of very attractive flooring materials. Either a terrazzo floor or a tile floor can be a positive selling point for any interested buyer.

I have seen indoor/outdoor carpet used as a base for indoor cages and aviaries, but this material is not satisfactory for a variety of reasons. Indoor/outdoor carpet will collect all of the dirt, dust, seeds and hulls that the birds scatter, and even a powerful vacuum may not be adequate enough to keep this type of carpet reasonably clean and attractive. Should you ever remove the aviary, this carpet will need a professional cleaning to restore it to its original, attractive color and texture.

Concrete flooring is another possibility as a flooring for the indoor aviary, of course, but again concrete has some disadvantages that I have mentioned for outdoor aviaries in other chapters. Unless the concrete flooring you use is very smooth and well sealed, it will stain easily, and it will be impossible to keep clean and attractive. Even a well sealed concrete floor is less than satisfactory, because water and bird droppings will make the sealed concrete very slippery.

For using the floor as an aviary base, you can still put pine needles or some other clean material over any of the flooring types that have been discussed here. This floor covering will make the flooring into a more natural base for the birds. Birds are not at home on any type of a slick or slippery surface, as the natural soil that they are used to has a much softer and more uneven texture. Any material that you can scatter over the flooring to form a more natural base will certainly make the birds feel more at home in the indoor aviary.

You can place the feeding station for the birds you keep in the indoor aviary at any location that is convenient for your daily maintenance and replenishment. Just keep in mind that the hopping and flying of the birds scatters the seed, the seed husks and dust widely. Placing the aviary food containers so that the scattered food is still available to the birds will be an important consideration.

Also, as there is no danger from weather or predators in the indoor aviary, you can place the birds' nesting receptacles wherever there is adequate space. Give the birds a variety of nesting sites, some of which are relatively hidden, and the pairs will choose the location that pleases them. Then, hopefully, they will commence their breeding cycle. Though most birds will accept dried grasses as nesting material, one of the cleanest and best materials you can use for this purpose is coconut fiber. This is available from several commercial suppliers of bird supplies. A company with the name RoLanka International, Inc., supplies this coconut fiber in bundles at a very reasonable price, reasonable enough that the shipping will probably cost you more than the actual coconut fiber costs.

The water supply for the indoor aviary needs a little more attention. As sure as the sun rises, the birds will splash and scatter water as they drink and bathe. Because of the mess that this can make, it might be best to place the water container on a piece of glass or Plexiglas that you place on the floor under it. A piece of this impervious material will go a long ways toward protecting the floor under the aviary, especially when you have placed the aviary over hardwood flooring. A wide variety of water containers is available, and you will have to choose the one that will serve you and your indoor aviary most effectively.

One of the best types of water container to use, as I have mentioned in other chapters, is one of the commercial, galvanized poultry waterers. These are reasonably cheap, readily available at any feed store or farm store, they hold enough water for several days, and they are easy to clean and disinfect when that becomes necessary. You can clean and refill them easily in the bathtub in the nearest bathroom. Any type of continually running fresh water system that you could use for the indoor aviary is going to be more trouble than it is worth. Unless you're establishing a huge bank of aviaries in a large warehouse, a system of running water is a needless expense. It will be much easier to use a simpler water container for your indoor aviary in the home.

The greatest disadvantages inherent in the indoor aviary are the constant sources of dust. This dust comes from three primary sources: the feathers of the birds, the droppings of the birds, and the seeds and other foods. Anyone who keeps birds indoors needs to be aware of these sources of dust and to take measures to minimize the accumulation of dust in the aviary and the spread of that dust from the indoor aviary all through the house.

The first primary source of dust develops when the feather grows from its feather follicle. The new feather is enclosed in a protective sheath. Once the feather is near maturing, the sheath breaks open and progressively crumbles and deteriorates as the feather completes its growth and frees itself. As the sheath disintegrates to free the growing feather, it creates a great deal of dust. An aviary of heavily molting birds is bound to be a dusty aviary.

The birds' droppings are also a major source of the dust in any indoor aviary. When the droppings become dry, they are crushed by the birds' normal activities. These crushed droppings form a fine powder that will become airborne with any flight or other activity on the part of the birds. This not only pollutes the air, but will also form a caustic layer on any surface in the house. This layer of corrosive dust will deteriorate many materials rapidly.

The seeds and other foods are a third source of dust in the indoor aviary. For the birds that shell their seeds, the seed husks and dust from the seeds are potent sources of dust. If you doubt that, just check the interior bottom of the feed dish after the birds have eaten out of it for a few days. There will be a thick layer of dust and fine particles in the bottom of the dish. All foods contribute to this dust when they are dry, though the commercial crumbles are certainly worse than the other foods in this regard. Most aviary birds generate this food dust in unbelievable amounts. The small doves and quail are exceptions to this, as they eat their seeds whole and without shelling. This will prevent the accumulation of seed husks in the aviary. However, even when you keep only doves and quail, you will not be able to lessen the amount of dust that is inherent in any bag of mixed seed.

109

Controlling the dust and feathers that are generated by the birds will be your greatest challenge in setting up and maintaining an indoor aviary. This dust is bad enough when kept confined to the room in which you have placed the indoor aviary. However, unless you have a well sealed door that will keep the mess confined to this one room, these avian by-products will sift through the entire house and will make your housecleaning a major task, indeed. The type of entrance to the aviary room that will create the highest house maintenance chore is an open entranceway without a door of any kind.

In order to keep most of the dust and feathers within the aviary, you will have to put some extra effort into the indoor aviary. The first possibility for reducing dust in the area near the aviary is through the use of an electrically powered air cleaner. There are several varieties of these on the market, and the cheapest ones circulate the air through a simple filter that must be removed and cleaned or replaced periodically. With the amount of dust that an aviary or birds can create, in most cases this will mean daily maintenance. Once the fine bird dust clogs the air filter, it will cease to perform its function and you are just wasting energy by running the air cleaner with a clogged filter.

The more modern and also the more expensive models of air cleaners use an electrostatic air filter that makes use of an electrical field to trap the dust particles in the air. This type of 'filter' many be simply an electrically charged surface that can be wiped clean with a damp cloth periodically. In some of the available air cleaners, this electrically charged surface is an actual metallic filter that you must remove and wash clean whenever it becomes coated with dust.

An alternate method of reducing the dust that goes from the indoor aviary into the house is by covering the aviary with a layer of either glass or Plexiglas. Either of these clear materials will be impermeable to dust and will still let the light that the birds need pass through and into the indoor aviary. However, either glass or Plexiglas in this quantity can become rather expensive when you are covering the entire surface of a reasonably large indoor aviary.

Small aviaries that are commercially made use these clear materials both to keep the birds within the enclosure and to keep the dirt and dust within the aviary. These small aviaries are rather expensive, but they truly qualify as furniture, rather than simply as a small aviary. A variety of styles and finishes make these small commercial indoor aviaries suitable for the living room in any home, with stained and polished wood framing and decoration. The glass or Plexiglas is installed in a double layer, so that one layer may be removed for cleaning, leaving the other layer to keep the birds enclosed within the aviary. These small commercial aviaries also have a built in light source that keeps the aviary well lighted at all times to show off the birds within to their best advantage. If you just want a small aviary or flight cage with a couple of pairs of birds in the house, these furniture quality commercial aviaries may be just what you need.

Chapter 14

Concluding Comments

This book has covered the planning and construction of an aviary in great detail, and has presented all of the information that you will need to establish a successful aviary under any normal conditions. Surely, you can ignore half of the recommendations that the author has made in these pages and still be quite successful in building an aviary and breeding exotic birds. However, never forget that Murphy's Law is lying in wait to cause you endless problems and disasters as you pursue your interests in the field of aviculture. The more tips you can make use of to prevent these problems and disasters, the better off you will be, and the more successful and healthy your birds will be.

As you have read through these chapters, you have undoubtedly noticed that some things have been covered in detail more than once. On some subjects, three different chapters will contain the same information, perhaps worded differently, but still essentially the same information. Be aware that this repetition is purposeful. It is not accidental, nor a case of inattention nor senility. Nor does this repetition expand the length of the book, as planning for the ending of a chapter often requires additional paragraphs to prevent the inadvertent creation of vast spaces of emptiness on a page. These subjects are the subjects that this writer considers to be the most important in the construction, maintenance and operation of any successful outdoor aviary. If you learn nothing else from this writing, study and learn well those subjects that have been repeated in more than one chapter. Those subjects are the very basis of success when you are keeping birds in an outdoor aviary.

As I have mentioned more than once in the preceding chapters, this world that we live in is a world of cause and effect. There are no such things as 'accidents' as every occurrence placed under such an innocuous label is an effect, and as such, it had a definite and direct cause. People would become more aware of the causes for such occurrences if they were called 'causatives' instead of 'accidents'. Labeling such happenings as 'accidents' tends to make us deny that there was a definite cause, and that line of thinking is totally at variance with the basic laws of this physical Earth. If you will keep in mind that everything that happens to you was not an accident and did not 'just happen', but had a definite and definable cause, you will be far better prepared for a life of experience on this physical world.

If one of your birds dies, it doesn't 'just happen'. There has to be a cause of death. In my other writings, I have covered dozens, perhaps hundreds of those causes. Some causes are as clear as crystal, as when a snake squeezes into your aviary and eats your birds. Others are obscure in the extreme, as when a bird just slowly sickens and dies, despite any effort we can make on its behalf. A secure aviary will go a long ways towards ending many of the causes of sudden death. A serious study of the nutritional needs of the birds and the foods that contain those nutrients will also be of inestimable value in ending many of the causes of slowly progressing illness and eventual death.

Thoughts are things. That simple fact is so misunderstood and ignored in our modern society that it is now virtually unknown to most people. Yet, the lack of this knowledge does not invalidate the premise. Your every thought goes out to influence your life and the lives of your birds and your successes or failures with them. Positive thoughts will bring positive results into manifestation. Negative thoughts will bring negative influences and occurrences. The power of positive thinking has been studied in detail, and there can be no doubt that your positive thoughts are among the primary factors that result in your success in all areas of human endeavor.

Thoughts are the most powerful things that exist in our human spheres. Never forget that everything, *everything*, that we know and use in our human civilizations was first of all a thought in someone's mind. This applies to the simple wooden peg as surely as it applies to a jet airliner or to a hydroelectric dam. Through the many years of my life, I have become convinced that this is the primary reason that our Creator has placed us on this Earth -- we are learning to think, and to transform those thoughts into physical objects and physical things. Of course we make mistakes, since our mental makeup dictates that we learn best from our mistakes, rather than from our successes. Simply by reading this book, you can get a very good idea of all of the mistakes this writer has made over the years in birdkeeping.

Instinctive fear serves a definite purpose in warning us to avoid danger and dangerous situations. However, chronic fear that is always present with no real basis for that emotion falls into a completely different category. Though fear is not the most destructive of emotions, it is a guarantee of negative results. Chronic fear acts as predictably as a magnet draws iron, and fear will draw directly to you those things or happenings that you fear most. Your fear of failure will guarantee that you will fail. Your fear of robbery will guarantee that you will be robbed. Should you find yourself fearing some specific occurrence, stop and change your way of thinking immediately. If you fail to do this, you will draw that which you fear directly to you.

Time and again in these pages, I have mentioned the twin characteristics that are the most important factors in any successful endeavor. These two factors are patience and perseverance. It takes a great deal of patience to deal with birds under avicultural conditions. As much as we love all of the birds in our care, they can be exasperating, frustrating, disheartening, and even disgusting at times. You must have the patience to deal calmly and gently with these occurrences when they happen, or else you will not have the patience to be a bird keeper and aviculturist over the long term. Patience is the characteristic that allows you to wait calmly for success, though that may take years with some species of birds that we keep. The patience you develop in caring for your birds will serve you well for the rest of your life.

Perseverance is that positive quality that keeps you working on something and improving on it, no matter how many failures and false starts you may have along the way. Though some may use the word stubbornness for this quality, a stubborn person can be stubborn either in a positive or a negative sense. Positive stubbornness is perseverance, and keeps you trying new things until something succeeds. Negative stubbornness will prevent a person from trying anything new, viewing what already exists as the best that is possible.

When it comes to bird keeping and aviculture, perseverance will keep you working towards a goal despite any breeding failures, losses, or natural disasters along the way. Those who completely give up after one or two tries are sorely lacking in this vital quality. As with most positive human attributes, anyone can develop a much higher degree of perseverance by just setting their mind to it. Nothing you attempt will ever be accomplished unless you can develop the ability to stick with it until it succeeds.

*   *   *   *   *

All living things have an energy field within and around them. Many books call this energy field the aura. Human auras are particularly large and colorful. As one psychic told me: "We are huge, and incredibly beautiful beings that have been stuffed into these little physical bodies to get the vital experience that is available only here on this physical Earth." All living things have this aura, and the development of Kirlian photography has managed to catch the beauty and diversity of the auras of energy that represent the life of any living thing.

If the birds you are maintaining are in perfect health, but making no attempt to breed, do not be adverse to trying unorthodox methods in your attempts to succeed with them. At one time, I was keeping three pairs of Brazilian Red-crested Cardinals, *Paroaria coronata*, each pair in a separate aviary with a few other compatible birds, such as Diamond Doves, *Geopelia cuneata*, Cape Doves, *Oena capensis*, and Green-winged Doves, *Chalcophaps indica*. After over a year, these cardinals still had made no nesting attempts in the aviary. As one of my local friends was a very gifted psychic, I asked him to look at the birds and see if he could get any kind of feeling for the sexes of the pairs or what was wrong that they were making no breeding attempts. When he looked at the cardinals and felt their life energy, he assured me first of all that I did have three true pairs. This was no minor piece of information, as these cardinals are notoriously difficult to sex.

At that point, I asked him, "If they're true pairs, can you get any feeling as to why they aren't breeding?"

He closed his eyes and again felt the birds' energy, then said "They want a rotten log."

"A rotten log?? Why in the world do they want a rotten log?"

"I haven't the foggiest idea -- I just see them perching on and digging into a rotten log. Give them a rotten log and see what happens."

Fortunately, the aviaries were next to a forested area, so I searched out three rotting logs and dragged them into the aviaries. Though I never saw the cardinals even perch on the logs in those aviaries, within two weeks, all three pairs of the Red-crested Cardinals had built nests in the laurel oak trees in their aviaries and they were all sitting on fertile eggs.

*   *   *   *   *

Another thing that many of us forget is that a large number of the species that we keep in our aviaries come from south of the Equator, either from Australia and its nearby islands or from central and southern Africa. South of the Equator, the seasons are the reverse of ours here in the Northern Hemisphere. Spring comes in September, and that is the time of the year when these Southern Hemisphere birds would normally breed. A prime example is the Lady Gouldian Finch, *Chloebia gouldiae*. Though the mutations and color varieties of these birds will often breed successfully at any time of the year, the birds of the original, wild colors usually will only begin breeding in the months of August, September or October, and then will continue through our Northern Hemisphere winter. Anyone who tries to change this breeding pattern to correspond to spring in the Northern Hemisphere is unlikely to raise many Gouldian Finches. Be prepared to accommodate your birds from the Southern Hemisphere when they show signs of coming into breeding condition in September and October. The Gray Singing Finch, *Serinus atrogularis*, and the Green Singing Finch, *Serinus mozambicus*, also are most likely to breed during these autumn months. Give them aviaries that are warm enough and light enough to encourage their breeding efforts during our fall and winter seasons here in the Northern Hemisphere.

Another factor that is a prime stimulation for birds of the dryer climate areas is the coming of the rainy season. The rains foster the growth of all of the grasses and other plants. The rains also stimulate the breeding and life cycles of the many varieties of insects that are native in these areas. All of this means a plentiful food supply for feeding a nest of growing young ones, and consequently, a period of rains is the time when many of our birds will come into breeding condition very rapidly. Be aware of the stimulating effect that rain storms have on many of your birds and have everything available that they need for breeding when the rainy periods occur. By providing nesting sites and a bountiful food supply at this time, you will be far more likely to raise many of the species that come from dry climate areas of the world.

*   *   *   *   *

In closing, I will leave you with these final thoughts. The more things you work with and attempt to learn while you go through life, the better off you will be, no matter what may happen in the future. The saying 'knowledge is power' was true yesterday, and it is true today, tomorrow, and forever. The more things you know and the more things you know how to do, the more respect you will earn from your fellow travelers though this school of life. We are incredibly fortunate to live in a time when literacy is so much respected and a time when books are available on any subject that you might care to learn. Once you have read a book on a subject that you've never known about nor understood before, you will be well on your way to complete understanding of the subject when you tackle that subject in reality.

Last, never forget that there is only one thing that you have that no one can ever take away from you. That is your knowledge. Anything else that you have can be lost, destroyed, stolen or killed, including your friends, your family, your home, your freedom and even your health, along with all of your physical possessions. But no one can ever destroy or take away your knowledge. If you believe in a life to come after you leave your physical body in death, believe also that the only thing you will take with you is your knowledge and your experience. That is the purpose of life on this physical Earth.

About the Author

Robert G. Black has always been interested in a number of occupational fields, but aviculture and horticulture have always been his primary interests. He has raised a variety of birds over the years, but has always specialized in the finches. In varying climate areas in Georgia, Florida, North Carolina, California, and Oregon, he has raised canaries, budgies, cockatiels, Fischer's Lovebirds, Quaker Parakeets, several species of doves, and many varieties of finches. Bob currently breeds Lady Gouldian Finches, and of course the commoner Zebras and Societies. He is also working with a variety of other finch species.

Bob consistently writes about his experiences with birds, and he has written many articles on finches and other cage birds for the national magazines over the last thirty years. His books and pamphlets include "Society Finches as Foster Parents", "Problems with Finches", "Nutrition of Finches and Other Cage Birds", "Establishing a Breeding Strain in Aviculture", "Cockatiels: Their Care, Feeding and Breeding", "Avian Nutrition", and "Building an Aviary". Also, Bob has compiled over sixty very specialized fact sheets on finches and other birds and their nutritional needs.

Bob now resides on a forested hillside in Keno, Oregon, shepherding the development of a large variety of fruit trees, nut trees, berries and many special ornamental plants that are resistant to browsing by the local animals. Now that he has the space and time, he is branching out to larger birds, such as pigeons, pheasants, ducks and chickens. Finches still remain the primary species that he breeds and keeps.